INDETERMINACY AND INTELLIGIBILITY

SUNY Series in Systematic Philosophy
Edited by Robert Cummings Neville

INDETERMINACY
AND INTELLIGIBILITY

BRIAN JOHN MARTINE

STATE UNIVERSITY OF NEW YORK PRESS

Published by
State University of New York Press, Albany

© 1992 State University of New York

Printed in the United States of America

Production by Cathleen Collins
Marketing by Dana Yanulavich

For information, address State University of New York
Press, State University Plaza, Albany, N.Y., 12246

Library of Congress Cataloging in Publication Data

Martine, Brian J. (Brian John), 1950–
      Indeterminacy and intelligibility / Brian John Martine.
          p.   cm. — (SUNY series in systematic philosophy)
      Includes index.
      ISBN 0-7914-1173-7 — ISBN 0-7914-1174-5 (pbk.)
      1. Determinism (Philosophy)   2. Ontology.   3. Relation
(Philosophy) I. Title. II. Series.
B105.D47M37 1992
123—dc20   91-38674
                                                                          CIP

10 9 8 7 6 5 4 3 2 1

For Cathy, David, and Christopher

CONTENTS

Acknowledgments

There are as usual far too many people to thank for their help during my work on this book, but I am particularly indebted to my colleagues, Andrew Cling, Frederick Elbert, Margaret Lang, and Daniel Rochowiak for reading the manuscript in whole or in part and offering many useful insights. For their advice at various stages while the project was brought to completion, I want to thank William Desmond, James Sheridan, and Carl Vaught. Through their friendship and support, Enda and Kevin Gill of Inis Mór have also contributed much more than they suppose. And finally, I owe a special debt of thanks to my friend Eleanor Hutchens for her patient advice and support throughout.

INTRODUCTION

European friends have often mentioned to me that they find it amusing that Americans are so much inclined to define themselves (and everyone else) in terms of "what they do." I don't know whether it is the typically American focus on things practical or simply a matter of curiosity, but I have certainly noticed this inclination in myself and my American friends. It is common practice to ask what people do almost at the same time as extending a hand in initial greeting. Or, with people one knows, to ask what they have been doing in particular since the last meeting. The point in mentioning this is that philosophers, at least in America, have a hard time making sense to most other Americans of just what it is that they do, and have to come up with some sort of standard speech that will work as a response at cocktail parties and on airplanes. This isn't an easy thing to do.

Of course, in some areas of philosophy, it's easier than in others. If one is working on ethical issues, say, or aesthetics, or some other fairly clearly defined area, it's not hard to give someone a reasonable idea of what the work amounts to inasmuch as it touches on a part of nearly everyone's experience in a fairly direct way. But if one's chief interests lie where my own do, it is much more difficult. In recent years, I have decided to bite the bullet and tell people that what I do is metaphysics. Nine times out of ten, this has the advantage of halting any further inquiry, but one does occasionally come across someone either sufficiently stubborn or sufficiently bored to demand an explanation of what that is supposed to mean. And there's the rub. Because there is really no agreement even among philosophers about just what this means, it is next to impossible to come up with a response that will make sense to people outside the world of professional philosophy. I sometimes tell people that it is something like the kind of thing that theoretical physicists do, with the difference that philosophers use natural rather than mathematical language, and let it go at that. But while that is a reasonably accurate claim, it's not very helpful.

The trouble is that doing metaphysics, whatever the particular area of inquiry, always means thinking about issues from the broadest possible perspective. And in an age increasingly devoted to narrow specialization in both theory and practice, this means rather swimming against the stream. Systematic inquiry just isn't much in fashion, and hasn't been for some time. In fact, to the extent that people are thinking about systematic philosophy at all these days, it is generally with the deepest suspicion. And I am by no means unsympathetic to their concerns. My own work began as a reaction against what I took to be the chief drawback of the modern drive toward a complete and systematic account of human experience. As my education in the Western tradition progressed, it began to seem to me that there was no place for the individual in a tradition that had, after all, been conceived and developed by individuals. To be scientific was to deny one's own voice, and one's own experience. The true is the universal, I learned; the individual, where it appears at all, should be played down and if possible, removed from one's reflection altogether. Time enough to return to the individual when we have the serious notions straight. Time enough to return to the nitty gritty of human experience when we have woven our reflective nets carefully enough so that what's truly interesting about it can be captured and examined.

I thought then as I do now that there is danger here. We become too easily attached to the creatures of our own reflection and begin to suppose that the aspects of concrete experience that elude capture are probably unimportant anyway, something to be dismissed like the "sports" of Aristotelian biology. Soon we spell out the grand systems, those elaborate and elegant frameworks that seem to hold the key to all knowledge, ways of thinking that will lead not only to complete understanding but to complete harmony, since of course, from the beginning, we have been inclined to suppose that the two are bound together. If there is something disharmonious here or there, some scrape or squeak, some overtone that strays far enough to disturb the glassy surface of the symphony, we assume that it will be smoothed out on the next reading. Surely in the end, everything will give itself over to the clear tones of the theme that we stated in the beginning; the final resolution will swell with the grandeur and closure of the major chord tentatively stated at the outset. But we give the final performance only to find that somewhere, somehow, something has been left out. The music is empty. The last chord, however magnificently conceived and articulated, is finally the abstract expression of an experience that it cannot contain, since it is after all only *an* expression of that experience, not *the* expression. The individuals by whom the work is executed and for whom the work is originally conceived cannot be neglected if the work itself is to continue to have any meaning.

But it is not enough merely to mention that individuals, or more broadly, the individual dimensions of human experience, have been neglected by the tradition. Unless this amounts to a *logical* mistake, it might after all be argued that individuality can be dismissed along with some of the other more obvious illusions of direct experience. In *Individuals and Individuality,* I tried to show that it *is* a logical mistake, and one that leads to a serious lacuna even in what is represented as the most complete of all rationalistic systems, Hegel's conception of the progress of Absolute Spirit. A brief summary of those arguments and the conclusions that I reached appears in the beginning of the first chapter of this book. The reason for mentioning them here is that the chief logical argument of this book developed directly out of my earlier thinking about individuals and universals and the ontological relations that define and sustain them. While working with those relations, it became more and more clear to me that making a place for the individual in systematic reflection meant abandoning the notion of an utterly complete system. The immediacy of the relation (or mode of being) that sustains the individual dimensions of experience stands against the mediated categories of traditional reflection in a way that cannot itself be mediated. As a result, an opening or gap is introduced into the circle of systematic reflection as it has been traditionally conceived. In the end, I found that my objection to Hegel—whose system is in my view the best of the attempts to close the circle—was not that he was too comprehensive in his understanding of experience, but rather that he was not comprehensive enough. His view of intelligibility, following the presuppositions and biases of the Western tradition, is too narrow. I think now, and shall argue in what follows, that this is the result of a lopsided focus on the determinate dimensions of direct and reflective experience. Nor is this a critique that applies to Hegel and the rationalistic tradition alone, but one that I think must be lodged against the Western tradition as a whole.

When I was first working on *Individuals and Individuality,* I thought that I was delving into the most fundamental of all ontological terms by taking up a consideration of the relation between individuals and universals. Since that time, I have come to think that while the relation that preoccupied me for so long has indeed a fundamental character, it is actually one that depends upon another whose roots lie still deeper in the ontology of our tradition. The notion of the determinate, that is, of the limited, the bounded, or the defined, lies at the foundation of all of our thinking as a natural function of the way that we think. In fact, I believe that it is a necessary function of the way that we think. Confronted by a world filled with seemingly endless variety and pervasive movement, we struggle to mark out boundaries that will somehow make sense of a confusing forming and reforming of elusive appearances. However, these boundaries are not self-sustaining. The lines that we draw as we form categories and classes, principles and laws, are drawn always against the background of direct experience. They are drawn by contrast with the indeterminate shapes and contours of a world that will continue to resist any effort to completely confine it within the determinately structured bounds of traditional reflective schemes.

In what follows, my central concern is to show that the relation between the determinate and indeterminate dimensions of our experience precludes any attempt to restrict our conception of intelligibility to the determinately biased models that we have used in the past. And, as I shall demonstrate, this is as much a logical as it is an experiential claim. We must open ourselves to a new understanding of understanding itself, making a place for a certain indeterminacy even in those regions of reflective thought that have heretofore been seen as the most clearly and precisely defined. Showing that this is the case requires careful and deliberate exposition, and I shall not try to anticipate those arguments here. However, it seems to me that it would be useful at this stage to make at least a few comments about the course that my reflection has taken thus far, and about where it seems to be leading next.

It may seem otherwise, but as I was first sketching the ideas that have taken shape in this book, the path I followed was a logical rather than an historical one. As I considered the logical foundations of the suggestions that I had made in *Individuals and Individuality,* it seemed best to try to return to the beginnings of logic itself, thinking through those first steps that developed into the ontology of the Western tradition. I was staying on Inis Mór, the large island of the Aran group off the west coast of Ireland, a place that had been inhabited long before that tradition found its legs. I began to think about the people who built the prehistoric fortresses on the island, about what their first attempts at logical thought might have produced, how their ideas might have been structured. It seemed obvious that the fundamental categories that the Milesians worked with would have occurred to those people as well, as they must occur still to someone looking out at the sea and the rocks, feeling the air as a palpable force, knowing that without fire, he could not survive. Standing up on that treeless cliff, awed by the power of the sea and the wind, rooted in the solidity of the rock beneath one's feet, warmed by the cloud-masked sun, those categories spring to life as the most fundamentally real of all things. And they spring to life as one. They work with and against one another to create the world. If some speech about that world is to be made, then, how better to form it than out of the same elements that mold its subject?

After having worked through some of the relations among these primitive categories as a way of thinking about much broader issues—determinacy, indeterminacy, intelligibility itself—it was particularly interesting to find that when I was recalled to an examination of Plato's struggle with the same issues, he had followed a similar path. I doubt that he was much more interested in the scientific viability of the Milesian scheme than I am, but as he tried to work out the logic of sameness and otherness, he also returned to those earliest categories, thinking his problem through in terms of the hot and the cold, the wet and the dry. Perhaps logic has a life of its own that always leads us down the same path. The path goes so far, and then returns to try to recapture its own ground. What I mean to offer here is something like an examination of logic itself, as presumptuous as that sounds. But it is not an examination like those of the last century's work that detail a careful analysis of the categories that we have all been manipulating with greater and greater facility through the ages. There is a deeper logic that we have not investigated with nearly enough care.

I remember an argument with an eminent analytical logician a few years ago, a futile argument as it turned out, in which I was trying to convince him that the categories that he was using to attack my suggestions about determinacy were already great leaps beyond the point that I was trying to make. He wanted to examine the claims that I was making using a bivalent logic that, as I tried to show him, itself depended upon much more primitive relations, not all of which give themselves over to the kind of analysis that such a logic makes available to us. The point that I intended to make was not that it is a mistake to use those analytical techniques, or to refine the categories that issue from them, but that the whole process depends upon a logical relation that undergirds our logical practice and that must be taken into account in our conclusions. If the very possibility of a determinate understanding of things depends upon an original and reciprocal play between determinacy and indeterminacy, the conclusions that we reach, however definite and precise they may seem as we articulate them, take on a rather different character when considered from the broadest perspective. The indeterminacy of our beginning reaches through the process to color and shape the whole in such a way that our reflective labor must always remain, at least in this sense, incomplete.

But this incompleteness is not a cause for despair. The notion that it should be possible to utter the last word, frame the final law, is after all only a notion. It is itself an idea that has a history, and like other ideas, it may well fade away in the face of new concerns in theory and practice. I believe that we live at one of the most exciting times of human history, one of those times when we find ourselves confronted with the possibility of change in some of our most fundamental ideas. As I talk to colleagues at work in the arts, the sciences, in philosophy, there seems more and more a common sense that this is a time of ground breaking, of a return to the beginnings for a reassessment and a fresh start. With my own return to the beginnings in this book, I hope to have laid open the possibility of a new way of thinking about some of what has seemed fragmented and disconcerted in contemporary developments. If the world of contemporary thought seems confusing at present, it may be no more than a function of trying to see new ideas through the lens of the old. It is high time that we remember that we are the creators of ideas, not merely their creatures, and that if the world seems obscure when viewed through one kind of lens, it may simply be time to invent another. When we find ourselves having trouble making sense out of things, there is as much reason to wonder about what "making sense" means as there is to wonder whether anything does.

Given all of this, I have undertaken to treat the central concerns of this book in a style of philosophical reflection that will at times seem to depart rather strikingly from the sort of discourse that most of us in the profession have been trained to adopt. I am deeply convinced that if we are to find solutions to the fundamental questions that are arising in different forms on both sides of the tradition, we must reform our understanding of the appropriate language and contexts within which those questions are to be taken up. Even those most concerned to argue that we have abandoned the concrete dimensions of direct experience in favor of a set of barren abstractions have themselves been too often inclined to state their objection and develop their positions in a language available only to a relatively small audience. We must resist the growing temptation to rely upon a private jargon that in the end obscures at least as often as it clarifies the most basic issues of philosophical reflection. Those issues arise now as they always have out of the concrete ground of direct experience; and it is to that experience itself, not a categorially constrained version of it, that we must try to return if there is to be any hope of new solutions to the oldest problems. This means that philosophical discourse must not only consider but *embody* the experience from which it emerges, thereby displaying to open view both the ends and the *beginnings* of philosophical reflection. In this sense, the style that I have employed in this book, the images that I have tried to evoke, are crucial elements of the argument itself; and I hope that they will encourage readers to seek out the concrete ground of their own reflection as we work together to shape a new language in which to reassess some of our oldest ideas.

CHAPTER 1

Relations, Indeterminacy, and Intelligibility

Le bon sens est la chose du monde la mieux partagée: car chacun pense
en être si bien pourvu que ceux même qui sont les plus difficiles à
contenter en toute autre chose n'ont point coutume d'en desirer plus
qu'ils en ont.

Descartes, Discours de la methode

I. THINGS IN RELATION

It was in reflecting on the nature of the individual that I first became interested in the status of relations in ordinary experience. As I tried to come to
a clearer understanding of the relation between individuals and universals, it
began to dawn on me that I had been focusing on the wrong things altogether. In fact, it began to seem to me that my mistake had been precisely
in focusing on *things*. I had started off, in a manner typical of the modern
tradition, assuming that some of the things in our experience are universals,
others individuals, and that in order to describe the relation between these
two primary entities it would be necessary to detail something like their
most fundamental characteristics. Here, of course, the underlying assumption was that they *had* some fundamental characteristics that could be described independently of their relations to one another. The relations that
stand between the individual and the universal could then, and only then,
be completely explored.

The problem I confronted was the same problem that every thinker has
had to come to terms with at some point. No sooner do we try to describe the
individual independently of the universal than we run into an apparently insurmountable problem: the words—any words—that are the basic tools of
the task we have outlined are themselves entities of a certain sort, or at least
signs that point to entities of some sort, and the entities that they are or to
which they point appear to be things that stand in direct logical contrast to

1

the entities one is trying to describe as independent. The only tools available to description are already biased in favor of the universal, and that seems to leave open only a couple of alternatives: one, the "individuals" that had originally been taken to have a fundamental character of their own really do not; or, two, they stand in principle outside the reach of discursive language and thought.

The reasons that neither of these alternatives seems acceptable are detailed in the first chapter of *Individuals and Individuality* and the search for some third alternative is the primary concern of the rest of the book.[1] Allow me to quickly retrace the steps that led to my suggestions concerning such an alternative. It is clear enough that, short of treating individuals as inaccessible to discursive thought, we are forced to admit that we cannot *think* about them independently of their relation to universals. The possibility that they cannot *be* independently of that relation arises quite naturally then as the ontological correlate of the logical point. Nor does this come as a surprise. To modify Whitehead's claim, it is certainly true that one branch of the Western tradition can be understood as a series of footnotes to Plato or at any rate as variations on an essentially Platonic theme; and although that lends a certain air of respectability to our ontological correlate, it provides at least as much reason for pause. We have been down that road before only to find that it can lead to a position just as unattractive as consigning the individual to the logical wasteland of bare particularity. Here, instead, the individual turns out on reflective consideration to amount to a sort of logical mistake, a function of the failure of naive consciousness to recognize the essentially universal structure that undergirds that which at first presented itself as self-contained.[2]

As I continued to work my way through this tangled web of relations between individuals and universals, (supposing as I did so that it was at least in principle possible to disentangle the two, exposing their discrete and independent characters), it began to seem more and more likely that some fundamental misconception was standing in the way of a solution. Is it really reasonable to imagine in the first place that the terms *individual* and *universal* refer to logical or ontological entities that can make any sense independently of their relations to one another? That is, if we begin by assuming that there are some things in experience that can be identified as universal and others as individual, we will always find ourselves confronted by the problem of how to construct a coherent logical framework that can draw them back together (hence making them accessible to discursive thought) without doing damage to the independent ontic and epistemic characters that we took

---

1.   Brian John Martine, *Individuals and Individuality* (Albany: State University of New York Press, 1984).

2.   Ibid., see esp. Ch. 2, "Hegel's Beginning."

as givens, as the fundamental elements of our account. The temptation, of course, is to take one or the other as more fundamental, thereby making it possible to discuss the relation between the two from the point of view of a single ontological ground. But this will only give rise to some version of the familiar difficulties that I mentioned a moment ago. Put in slightly different terms, if we take the individual as fundamental and reduce the universal to a derivative status, we fall into the traps common to various versions of nominalism, the most significant of which is that we cannot do so without calling the logical character of our own speech into question. On the other hand, if we take the route of the rationalists, positing the universal as fundamental, the individual ends in being reduced to an instance of this or that category (or perhaps a cluster of such instances), and we are brought up short by the concern that we have done violence to our direct experience of the individual by depriving it of the concretely resistant character that seems to lie at its very core.

We seem at this stage to be confronted by the most serious sort of dilemma. The course of our reflection has bifurcated, issuing in two quite different but equally unacceptable alternatives. Moreover, given our historical vantage point, it seems unlikely that much would be gained by some further exploration of these alternatives in the hope of discovering some solution that had eluded the finest minds of our tradition. (At this juncture, the thinly veiled intellectual despair of the "deconstructionist" critique becomes understandable, if no more palatable.) The most reasonable response, then, is a return to the point at which we began and a reassessment of the presuppositions that guided our movement away from that beginning. Now, as I've said, as I set out to consider the relation between individuals and universals, I initially assumed that each introduced its own character into the subsequent structure of the relation and, as a result, that the relations between the two could only be understood after having come to an understanding of those fundamental characters. In the end, it occurred to me that quite different conclusions might issue from taking the relation (or relations) between the two as prior, as giving rise to the "fundamental characters" we think to have identified when we speak of "individuals" and "universals."

Individuality and *universality*, it seems to me, actually refer to relations, or to what I called modes of being related in *Individuals*. When we speak of the individuality of this or that, we really mean to point to its resistance with respect to the very categories that we use to describe it when thinking of it as an instance of a universal. While there may at first appear to be a conflict here, there is actually nothing particularly unusual about thinking of the same object in both ways. We typically suppose, for example, that the fact that persons can be described in terms of various universal categories, physical, psychological, social, and so forth, does not in the least mean that they are reducible to those categories. Neither does the fact that the categories offer rather less than a "complete" account mean that they should be abandoned as inappropriate or useless. The persons whom we encounter in ordinary experience are both individual and universal in the sense that they participate in both unmediated (dyadically structured) and mediated (triadically structured) relations to what they are not. Problems arise only when we begin to insist from some reflective vantage point that one or the other of these manners of being related must be given pride of place. As I argued at some length, there is no reason whatever for doing so, unless we suppose that there is something unshakeable about our modern presuppositions concerning the character of intelligibility—but of course, if we suppose that, philosophy comes to a halt.

Unsettling as that thought might be, however, there is something even more nervous-making about so radical a shift in our thinking as to imagine that relations might be prior to the things described in terms of them. For centuries now, we have been accustomed to assume that *things* occupy a status both ontically and epistemically prior to that of *relations among things*. If it is possible to speak intelligibly of relations per se, it has seemed reasonable to suppose that there must first be things that stand in relations and that such things at least from a logical point of view can be considered the bases of the relations we are trying to define. We move from relations like "being next to," "on top of," or "between," to being "similar to," "different from," "identical with," and so on. The things that are seen as standing in such relations are taken to be self-identical givens that the relations simply help to describe. But when we examine this sort of description, we encounter a difficulty logically similar to that which arises when we try to describe individuals using universal terms. Everything that we say about the objects that we had intially taken to be prior calls our attention to the relations in which those objects stand to the other objects around them. We find ourselves having to describe these "prior" *things* by means of relational frameworks of one kind or another, and in the process, the possibility of seeing the relations themselves as prior emerges as a serious one.

What could it mean to think of relations as prior? At first the suggestion seems counterintuitive; and while many of the "givens" of common sense expose themselves on closer examination to lead to unacceptable logical consequences, others appear so fundamental to our ordinary modes of thought that calling them into question seems tantamount to calling intelligibility itself into question. If, for example, we tried to suggest that the spatial relations of direct experience occupy a position either logically or ontologically prior to the things we are accustomed to think of as sustaining these relations, we would end in making some very curious claims. Surely, my computer and the table on which it rests are prior to the relation between the two. (Now we are not speaking of the sort of self-sustaining individuals with which we began; but by beginning with individuals in the sense of individual objects in ordinary experience, it will become possible eventually to show how some simple claims made in this context hold even more clearly in the case of such complex and full-bodied individuals as, say, works of art.) We naturally think of the computer and the table as prior to the ordinary spatial relation "on top of" in the sense that the computer and the table do not stand in any necessary relation to one another. That is, the computer would obviously be what it is if put in other places—on top of other tables, in the closet, on the floor, and so forth. It would still be the same object in the sense that it could be placed on a table and used in the way that it is being used now. To assign a certain independence to the thing, then, means at least that it has a meaning independent of the particular place in which it is situated at the moment. And, of course, it is true that its relation to this table is coincidental. The same sort of thing can obviously be said of the table, and it seems to follow that the relation between the two is something, far from being that on which they depend in any important sense, that depends on the objects for its meaning.

But if we continue to reflect on the apparent independence of the objects, it turns out that while this relation may be coincidental to what they are, it is not in the least clear that it would be possible to hold intelligibly that they are what they are independent of *any* relation whatever. Yet it is this that we often take ourselves to mean when we assert that the objects are prior to their relations to one another and to whatever else there may be. It is certainly true that most of the things we confront in ordinary experience (though not all) are independent of this or that set of relations, but can we really hold that they are ever independent of—here in the sense of being the sort of thing that can be thought separately from—relations in the more general sense? Think again of the assertion of the independent meaning of the computer. Are we really saying anything more than that it is possible to think of the object in terms of some set of relations other than the ones that currently apply to it? Well, if the only relations we consider are those that describe its connection with the other physical objects around it, of course we are. But review the other possibilities. Suppose we were to describe it as a unique collection of molecules. No matter how one tries to think of molecules, it is impossible to do so without becoming involved once again in a framework of relations, both internal and external to the structure of the entities. In fact, here the framework becomes even more complex in that it necessarily entails a reflective assessment of experience to the extent that molecules are obviously not a part of direct experience, and such an assessment carries along with it the usual set of presuppositions, categorial structures, and so on. When we turn from the theoretical back to the experiential and try to describe the computer in terms of the colors, shapes, textures, that seem to apply to it, we find ourselves once again confronted by a series of relations. Attending to its function will lead us, if anything, more directly down the same path. Its function distinguishes it from some objects, but does so only by drawing it into relation with others: keyboards, monitors, human hands, needs, abilities, and so on.

To be known as a this or a that, the computer has to be considered in terms of this or that set of relations. After only a brief reflection of this sort, one becomes less and less inclined to see those sets of relations as coincidental to the meaning of the object, but the notion that the object is something prior to all of them lingers still. What then? Perhaps an individual. That is, while all of the things that we think about the object entail its relation to things that it is not, isn't there still some sort of thing about which we are thinking, something that is independent of the things we think about it? The computer is not only *a* computer; it is also, and importantly, *this* computer. To say this, however, turns out to mean simply to point to another of the relations in which it stands to other things. This relation, as I have shown elsewhere, stands significantly apart from relations of the sort described earlier, in that its foundation is negation as opposed to difference, but it is a relation all the same.[3] What I am more interested in at the moment, though, is the way that the apparently determinate relations that detail the universal dimensions of our ordinary experience of the computer are connected to the indeterminate ground out of which they arise, and what that means with respect to the relation between indeterminacy and intelligibility in more general terms. Using the term *ground* may be misleading. I should like to make it clear at the outset that in doing so, I do not mean to present indeterminacy as having a more fundamental status than determinacy. However, I do want to insist that a certain indeterminacy surfaces in any reflection on determinately structured relations as something without which they would not make sense.

Imagine describing the computer to someone unfamiliar with objects of this sort, but familiar enough with the culture of which it is a part to make sense out of the various determinations (spatial location, molecular structure, physical characteristics, function) mentioned earlier. The relation between those determinations and what I have just characterized as their "indeterminate ground" might be drawn into better focus by considering the mistakes people might make if left to their own devices. Say we choose to develop our description of the computer primarily in terms of its function. To do so successfully, we should have to separate from all the possible uses to which one might imagine such an object being put, the use to which it actually is put. That is, we should have to take into account, either implicitly or explicitly, the various mistakes that might be made concerning its use. Doing so, however, does not eliminate the other possibilities in either a prac-

---

3. Ibid.

tical or theoretical sense. The computer could conceivably be used in a variety of other ways (stopping a door, say), or, to put the point (which is hardly a new one) more broadly in practical terms and more directly in logical terms, its definition depends as much on what it is not as it does on what it is. It is in this sense that the rationalists are right. The thing is tied to a larger set of things than it appears to be from the point of view of sense-certainty; and even if we deny the claim that it can ultimately be resolved into some determinate set of such relations, we cannot deny the importance of the discovery that we have made. It depends on what it is not in a fundamental way. But the rationalistic tradition has consistently neglected the extent to which the indeterminacy of what it is not enters into the determinate characterizations that we ordinarily provide in our attempt to come to an understanding of the thing.

The point I mean to emphasize is that when we examine the determinations that seemed from the point of view of naive consciousness to isolate the object in the sense of uncovering a meaning that it has for itself (i.e., that is independent of our reflection on it), we find that those determinations, far from separating the object from the larger context of which it is a part, draw it into closer and closer connection with it. So far we seem to be with the rationalists, and one of the possible conclusions available at the stage we've reached is theirs. We could expand our original notion of the determinations that structure not only the object in question but any object whatever, as they structure the Whole. But to do so involves an unsatisfactory reduction of the experience with which we began just to the extent that none of the possible descriptions mentioned earlier, theoretical or experiential, can be seen as in and of itself determinate. Even if we are willing to make the difficult move toward accepting the notion that the relations that emerge as the primary meanings of those descriptions are more fundamental than the relata appropriate to the respective contexts, various conflicts appear that seem to refuse the completely determinate character of a rationalistic superstructure.

There is a real difference, for example, between describing the computer as a collection of molecules, on the one hand, and in terms of its function in a human world, on the other. For one thing, the first sort of description presupposes an analytical approach to the world of ordinary experience, whereas the other certainly need not rest on such a presupposition and on some accounts might be seen as standing insistently against analysis. (If the computer really is its use, to think of the thing in terms of a collection of molecules is to think of something other than the computer.) Ignoring for the moment the wide variety of disputes that might arise within the camps of adherents to either view, imagine an argument between a committed materialist and an equally committed rationalist. Although such people seem ready to claim that the opposing view is "wrong," what they mean when they do so is always rather puzzling. The problem appears, of course, when one side or the other insists that they have identified what the object *really* is. If the object is really (i.e., at the most fundamental level) a collection of molecules, then its place in a world of intersubjective meanings and activities takes on a secondary role with respect to an understanding of the thing. Bugles sound, and the other camp is up in arms. What do you mean by suggesting that . . . ? But isn't it equally as unreasonable to try to hold that the computer is not really a collection of molecules as that it is? Or that one or the other of the two possibilities we are considering must be seen as secondary? That the physical objects of ordinary experience can be described in terms of their molecular structure is obvious. We do so. Moreover, we have been doing so with extremely impressive results for some centuries now. To argue that it is a mistake to describe the thing in these terms is simply ludicrous. But it is just as ludicrous to insist that on offering such a description we have come somehow closer to the real meaning or being of the thing than we do when we think of its place in ordinary human experience.

If a child walked into my office just now, pointed to my computer, and asked "What's that?," I should scarcely respond by telling him about its molecular structure. Nor, on describing its operations and functions, would I understand myself to be reserving the real truth about the thing until he was old enough to understand it. In fact, it seems to me that to tell him that it is a collection of molecules would be to make a mistake. That is not the sort of thing he was asking me about. To genuinely understand the object is not only to understand that both of these descriptions apply to it, but also to understand the context within which each becomes useful and meaningful. Each description can, from a certain point of view, be seen to conflict with what the object means and is when considered from other points of view. For example, its place in the world of intersubjective human experience does not quite come apart into discretely meaningful pieces in the way that its molecular structure does. And to assume that there must be some complete and thorough resolution to such conflicts is to ignore the indeterminacy that enters the picture with the contextual variety that has emerged as fundamental to the meaning of the object. Not only is it the case that some of those contexts are themselves indeterminate, but likewise that the relations between those that are determinate and those that are indeterminate must remain itself indeterminate. But this is a sort of indeterminacy that we are ordinarily inclined to accept quite happily. Actually, it never occurs to us to think that the indeterminacy of our experience stands in conflict with the claim that the world is intelligible until we start doing philosophy. Quite to the contrary, in fact, indeterminacy figures strikingly in a variety of experiences that we should never dream of characterizing as unintelligible. Let me try to develop this claim by turning to a context in which it is not only difficult to hold that intelligibility is fundamentally tied to determinacy, but clearly a mistake to do so.

II. INDETERMINACY AND INTERPRETATION

Not long ago, while still searching for a context particularly appropriate to an exploration of the relation between indeterminacy and intelligibility, I appealed to a friend who is a professor emerita of English literature. It seemed a good idea to settle on some single literary example as a method of attack, and she suggested Yeats's familiar poem, "Among School Children." Of course, this is not an example that came to mind entirely without reason. In the poem, Yeats is reflecting on his own experience, thinking about the relation between youth and age, what it means to have come to a new way of seeing the world, comparing it to ways in which he had once seen it. The poem has to do with just the sort of issue we had been talking about. That is, its images awaken in the reader a sense of returning to a beginning, considering its shape and texture not only in terms of the end that has in fact issued from it, but likewise in terms of those alternative ends that might have done. But the primary reason for considering this poem would apply just as well to any other good piece of poetry. That is, we are presented with something that must be seen as indeterminate in that it can be interpreted in not one but several perfectly reasonable ways. Furthermore, while the range of available interpretations is not without limits (since it is certainly possible to make mistakes), neither are its boundaries entirely determinate. What is particularly to the point here is that this is ordinarily seen as strengthening rather than weakening the claim that the poem is meaningful.

With that much said, let us take a more direct look at "Among School Children" itself. I hope that the poem is familiar enough that quoting the last stanza will be sufficient to recall its tone and imagery to mind.

> Labour is blossoming or dancing where
> Body is not bruised to pleasure soul,
> Nor beauty born out of its own despair,
> Nor blear-eyed wisdom out of midnight oil.
> O chestnut tree, great-rooted blossomer,
> Are you the leaf, the blossom, or the bole?
> O body swayed to music, O brightening glance,
> How can we know the dancer from the dance?

At the opening of the poem, Yeats finds himself in a schoolroom surrounded by a group of children involved in the elementary stages of education. He is naturally drawn to some reflection on the relation between his own youthful experience and the developed perspective of a "sixty year old smiling public man." Out of that reflection emerges a series of ideas concerning the passage from youth to age, the consideration of the early stages from the point of view of the later, the relative weight of this influence or that as it is considered from either the beginning or the end. Depending upon the reader's focus, the meaning of the poem might be seen to move in either direction or in both. Consider the lines just quoted. One might interpret the last two lines as meaning that the dancer is actually identical to the dance. For the "scarecrow" whose dance is nearly completed, the return to a schoolroom calls to mind the progress from youth to age, conjuring up images and relations that have become part of him in an internally necessary sense. He *is* his relationship with Maud Gonne (who is usually taken to be the woman of stanzas two through four), he *is* his early fascination with and later departure from the world-view of the classical Greeks, he *is* the spirituality both sacred and secular that enshrouds the images of the "nuns and mothers" of the seventh stanza. At the same time, he remains in some sense identical to the infant on the mother's lap, full of potential crying out for realization, though not necessarily for the particular realization that was to come. For the dance is not yet complete, and the dancer not after all identical to the dance. In fact, if he were, there could be neither dancer nor dance, and the image would collapse into meaninglessness.

But the emphasis to be placed on the one view or the other remains open to question. Is Yeats telling us that the view from the perspective of the nearly completed whole is to be taken more seriously than the view from the mother's lap? Less? A reasonable argument might be made in either direction. Or perhaps the most reasonable interpretation of the poem lies somewhere in between. Not "between" in the sense of a diffident vacillation between the two possibilities mentioned, but firmly between, where the meaning of the two directions is to be found in the curious relation between the indeterminacy of the one and the discrete determinations of the other. Perhaps we see the poem most clearly when we allow our focus of attention free rein, looking from end to beginning and beginning to end, recognizing that the play between the two draws us nearer to the truth than a narrowed focus in either direction could do on its own.

Or we might follow some other path altogether. It would not be wholly unreasonable, for example, to interpret the poem as a critique of a certain kind of formal education. There is some evidence supporting such an interpretation in the poem itself—the description of the children learning "to be neat in everything in the best modern way," the characterization of Plato, Aristotle, and "golden-thighed" Pythagoras as "old clothes upon old sticks to scare a bird." Further support for such a view appears on discovering that at the time Yeats was interested in Gentile's ideas concerning educational reform; and still other variations on both themes seem reasonable in light of the note concerning the topic of the poem that Yeats jotted down about three months before the completion of the final draft: "School children and the thought that life will waste them perhaps that no possible can fulfill our dreams or even their teacher's hope. [sic] Bring in the old thought that life prepares for what never happens."[4]

We might account for variations within the range of possible interpretations in a number of ways but the primary reason for such a range seems fairly obvious: the poem can be and is assessed from a variety of significantly different perspectives. If we cast our understanding of the poem in the mold formed by what we know of the poet and his experience prior to and contemporaneous with the writing of the poem, certain interpretations will seem more reasonable than others, but it would be odd to insist that those interpretations are more accurate than others. Further, even on narrowing our focus by choosing to adopt this perspective rather than others, we find that, although some interpretations are excluded (at least from immediate consideration), no single interpretation emerges as the only reasonable possibility. Imagine the course our reflection would take if we were, say, to approach "Among School Children" using the note quoted earlier as a point of departure. Because the note itself is open to a number of interpretations, we would first have to choose from among those possibilities the one that seems best suited in terms of what we know of Yeats's background, related interests, and so forth. That is, we should have to engage in a sort of second-order interpretive activity before it became possible to apply the note and our interpretation of it to the poem itself. Once having done so, we would find ourselves faced with still another series of decisions concerning the most reasonable application of the interpretation we have elected. Moreover, as many artists have pointed out, there comes a moment in the making of a work of art when the work seems to take on a life of its own, thereafter making demands on the artist that he or she might not have anticipated. To the extent that this is true of at least some works of art (Croce and others notwithstanding) and might well be true of the particular piece under consideration, it is perfectly reasonable to suppose that by the time "Among School Children" was completed, Yeats had departed in large or small ways from his original plan. In short, even after having adopted one of the various perspectives from which the poem might be considered, we still find ourselves offering an interpretation that no amount of argument could show to be the single best interpretation of the poem even from that perspective, let alone others.

So far, in thinking about the poem from the perspective of the ideas and experiences brought to the work by the poet, we have seen that such reflection would eventually produce a range of interpretations including some

---

4. A. Norman Jeffares, *A Commentary on the Collected Poems of W. B. Yeats* (Stanford, Calif.: Stanford University Press, 1968), p. 299.

that conflict with one another. Should we turn our attention to the various experience of the poem's audience, that range would obviously broaden enormously. Where the average college student might be inclined to focus on the romantic imagery in the center of the poem, allowing it to color his or her understanding of the beginning and end, that student's teacher, who has perhaps become a "sixty year old smiling public man," will have strikingly different notions about the poem's core. Enough. It is clearly possible to propose a wide range of reasonable and nevertheless significantly different interpretations of a poem like "Among School Children." Likewise, in the case of a genuinely important poem, that is to say one that will "last" and develop a history of its own, that range of interpretations will undergo constant change. That it provides a framework within which this can occur is in fact one of the things ordinarily taken as grounds for referring to it as "important."

Now, the poem is certainly intelligible in the ordinary sense of the term. It is open to meaningful interpretation. Its meaning, however, remains indeterminate at least to the extent that a variety of interpretations are available and choosing among them involves further interpretation. It is equally important to note how strange it would be to suggest that we approach the poem with a determinately formulated goal in mind. If we think of ourselves as seeking the "truth" about the poem at all, it is certainly not in the sense of hoping to ultimately identify the most clear and distinct of all the possible interpretations that might be offered. We seek, if anything, to constantly enrich our understanding of the poem by considering new ways of thinking about it in relation to the poet himself, his audience, the complex relation between the two, the history of its imagery, the extent to which its metaphors reshape ordinary conceptual links of this sort or that, the peculiar perspective it affords for a reconsideration of the past out of which it has emerged and the future at which it hints. At the same time, none of this is to suggest that any interpretation whatever would do. It is quite possible to make mistakes. In fact, one of the most obvious ways to do so would be to attempt to treat the poem in an overly determinate fashion, as if, for example, it were made out of parts in the way that a machine is. One imagines (if only with a shudder) some hard-bitten analyst zeroing in on the lines:

> O chestnut tree, great-rooted blossomer,
> Are you the leaf, the blossom, or the bole?

and trying to figure out which one it is. To attempt a formal analysis of the poem would be as silly—and a silliness of the same sort—as telling the child in the preceding section that the computer is a collection of molecules.

The poem seems to present us with an instance of something undeniably meaningful, but whose meaning has the character of being in one sense bounded and in another quite open. Or, to put the point in the language of the first section, the meaning of the poem appears to be at once determinate and indeterminate. And this raises once again the question of the relation between determinacy and indeterminacy. In the last section of this chapter, and in the chapters that follow, I shall explore the possibility that far from being an unusual case, the relation between the bounded and the unbounded uncovered in the meaning of the poem points to a logically necessary reciprocity between the determinate and indeterminate dimensions of the entire range of our experience.

III. DETERMINACY AND INTELLIGIBILITY

In the first section, I suggested that we would do well to reconsider the prior ontic and epistemic status we have been accustomed to accord to "things," on the grounds that some of the most perplexing problems with which we have struggled throughout the history of the Western tradition, and in particular during the modern period, appear to discover their logical roots in this presupposition. When we try to consider "things" while neglecting the significance of the relations in terms of which we describe them and by which they are structured, we doom ourselves to an unnecessarily restricted view of our own experience. At the same time, certain uncomfortable consequences seem to appear as soon as we shift the balance between things and relations in favor of relations. For it is not possible to raise doubts concerning the fundamental logical and ontological status of "things" without at the same time raising doubts about the pivotal ontological position of determinacy. The notion that determinacy should be taken to have such a status is so firmly lodged in the tradition that it seldom occurs to us even to raise questions of this kind, let alone to take them seriously. Yet, as I tried to show in general terms at the end of the first section and in particular terms in the second, it turns out that intelligibility does not always depend upon reaching a completely determinate conclusion. It is quite possible to reflect seriously, that is, to make intelligible claims, within and about contexts that are fundamentally indeterminate. And if this is the case, still another reassessment is called for. Something is amiss with the criteria we have been applying in making judgments concerning what is and what is not intelligible. Let me try to prepare the way for the following chapters with some general observations concerning the relation between determinacy and indeterminacy, and the importance of that relation for the structure of intelligibility itself.

Two or three years ago, a colleague asked me to make some remarks about the development of the scientific method as an introduction to her seminar in physiological psychology. Describing the roots of the method primarily in Cartesian terms, I was struck by the curious tension between determinacy and indeterminacy to be discovered with the method itself. There is scarcely any need to draw attention to the extraordinary success that we have had in learning more of the world and of ourselves as we have drawn this method into play in contexts both theoretical and practical. At the same time, I found myself anxious to convince my audience that while I had no interest in degrading either the theoretical structure or the practical efficacy of the method, it was nonetheless important to be wary of its hidden presuppositions.

To the extent that it is a method whose core is analysis, it is one that leads toward a view of human experience that can generate any number of significant misconceptions. For one, if we assume that we can learn most about things by analyzing them, we have to assume at the same time that the things about which we can learn are things that give themselves over to analysis; we must assume that they are things that come apart into pieces. Now of course, in ordinary experience, we confront almost nothing that can't be broken into pieces, but the further and more important underlying assumption here is that the pieces that are the necessary byproducts of analysis have independent meanings. Whether the pieces in question are molecules or natural laws, sense data or logical principles, they are invested with discrete meanings understood to stand independent of their relations to one another and to our experience of them. Nor is this in the least an unreasonable view when one considers the general character of our day-to-day experience. The things around me in the room as I write are things that certainly have meanings independent of those I am inclined to attach to them, and it is reasonable to suppose that they are made of smaller bits of which the same thing can be said. Here the move toward reflection on *my* world and the ways in which these objects have special meanings for me—my grandmother's violin, my friend's book, my parents' gift—seems to be beside the point. One thinks of learning to ask "But what is it really?" where of course the question directs one's attention away from the world of idiosyncratic tastes, familial sentiment, even some larger sense that grows out of a kind of general human sympathy, toward a world that has some meaning of "its own." This is the world of the "things" we considered in the first section. It is a world that we imagine transcending the merely personal and that, in becoming universal, becomes likewise more complete, more true, more real.

A hunger for that meaning that stands independent of oneself is typical of the whole tradition of Western philosophy. First gods, then natural phenomena, then ideal constructions, then God, then back to a combination of God, natural phenomena, and ideal constructions; round and round the search goes, always, it seems, with Thales's primary notion in mind: there must be something out of which everything else is made, there must be some fundamental meaning behind the appearances, if we are not to surrender ourselves to the more than just mildly disconcerting thought that the world we confront and try to come to terms with is merely whimsical. It is simply not acceptable. There must be a meaning. That this search is worthy of our time and effort, respect and sympathy, surely stands, if anything does, without argument. However, it cannot be carried out intelligently without a constant reappraisal of the extent to which the character of the search itself affects what we find.

When we treat analysis as the single most significant method of investigation, presupposing as we must that the world is made up of discretely meaningful bits and pieces, the conceptual structures in terms of which we articulate the relations among those pieces (principles, laws, meanings, etc.) are predestined to take on the same character as the pieces that we set out to look for in the first place. They must be determinate. When determination is seen as the primary model for thought, and likewise for being, that which appears indeterminate is taken to be intelligible (or, in an extreme view to be at all) only to the extent that it might approach some ultimate moment identified by the articulation of a determinate structure. When Descartes speaks of clarity and distinctness, he means to refer to just such a structure, and the frustration with which he repeatedly meets grows out of the sense that little or nothing in direct experience can be characterized in such terms.

The indeterminate comes to be seen now as an incompletely articulated version of the determinate. There is nothing inherently unreasonable in making such a suggestion. Its origins are in fact readily apparent. In both practical and theoretical contexts, success often depends upon becoming increasingly determinate in our understanding of various situations. Determinate forms emerge as the building nears completion, as the machine is further developed, as the mathematical proof is knitted together, even from a certain point of view, as the work of art coalesces; and in each case, the notion of accomplishing the task we have set for ourselves appears to involve more and more thoroughly defined structures. When we turn to reflection on such activities, isn't it reasonable to generalize, reaching the conclusion that human activity broadly defined involves a making-determinate?

But if we consider these activities from a slightly different angle, the apparently central character of this "making-determinate" can be seen to stand in a certain conflict with the notion that the determinations characteristic of the end products have been "discovered" rather than created. If for no other reason than that in each case some other end is possible at least in principle, the claim that the determinations we have come upon at the end of the process are not really ideal structures that were undergirding the process (together with everything else) from the outset seems more and more reasonable. Even in those contexts that seem most highly refined, a sense of the indeterminate lingers stubbornly. We can choose, of course, to put this aside as a function of not having enough control over our instruments and procedures, but in the case of direct experience that won't do simply because of the problem with the deceptive character of sense experience that has troubled us since the Presocratics. Even in the case of the mathematical system, it lingers penumbrally around the imaginary and transfinite numbers that seem necessary to the making-determinate of real numbers. (Or, one might just as well point to the existence of and relation between alternative systems, as specifically in the case of Euclidean and non-Euclidean geometries.)

The point in all of this is that if we shift our focus away from an insistence on the primacy of the determinate in both orders toward an inspection of the pervasive character of indeterminacy, it begins to seem just as reasonable to suppose that the determinate represents an inadequately articulated form of the potential represented by the indeterminate dimensions of experience. From this point of view, the indeterminate comes to the fore as the ground out of which the determinate systematic account has arisen in the first place and into which it will in a sense recede upon having outlived its usefulness. In fact, now the determinate is seen as incomplete. That which stood as the model for and the goal of the complete account is itself as incomplete as a single interpretation of a work of art.

IV. THE CONTEMPORARY LANDSCAPE

It may seem that in raising a question about the central place of determinacy, I have been focusing chiefly on the empirical side of the tradition, since it is the empirical branch of the modern tradition that most clearly and self-consciously accords analysis pride of place—and which as a result appears most obviously committed to the notion that being and thought are fundamentally tied to determinacy. But I believe that the same thing holds for the rationalistic tradition. In both of its central traditions, modern philosophy has until very recently continued to assume that intelligibility demands determinacy and that, where we uncover indeterminate dimensions in experience, it is chiefly to be understood as a sign that our thinking has not developed far enough, or that some aspect of the world is by nature elusive.

I say that this has been true until recently because there has been a movement afoot for the last several decades that seems not only to admit but to celebrate indeterminacy. Following in the footsteps of Kierkegaard and Nietzsche, this end of the contemporary philosophical landscape insists on the centrality of difference as against sameness, arguing that the world inevitably resists any attempt to confine it within clearly defined categorial boundaries. I am thinking of course of Heidegger's later work or, more recently, of Derrida and his cohort. I am in one sense quite sympathetic to the insights to be found in these positions, but the view that I am developing here remains importantly distinct from them. As I argued at length in the first part of this project, it does seem to me that we have lost sight of the importance of difference and of the place of the individual. At the same time, it is possible to get carried away in defense of these dimensions of experience, to become so involved in a focus upon difference that we lose sight of the sense in which the world does also present an orderly face and can, in a straightforwardly traditional sense, be known. We can, after all, legitimately construct categories and principles and laws on the basis of our direct experience inasmuch as that experience includes as much sameness as it does difference. It is no more reasonable to insist on an exclusive focus upon difference than it is to hold that sameness is somehow a more foundational or central notion.

Given my understanding of the relation between sameness and difference, and of its significance for the logical structure of the relation between determinacy and indeterminacy, the position that I shall be developing in this book seems to me to lie between two extremes, neither of which offers an adequate account of these relations. One of these extremes, represented by the sort of position just mentioned, is importantly identified with difference, arguing that difference lies at the very core of things, causing the world to be fundamentally enigmatic, shrouded in the mystery of the individual. Here, the world as a place of individuals and differing perspectives is taken to present a fundamental character that opposes our attempts to know. Heidegger, for example, seems to find in Being itself a natural propensity for difference. As against the Hegelian analysis, difference finally overwhelms identity for Heidegger, retreating into the "oblivion" (*Vergessenheit*) of a Being that remains concealed. Merleau-Ponty takes up a position not unlike this, especially in his later work where the Other both as the disjoined self and as a combination of an unrecoverable past and an unknowable future retreats from the immediacy of present experience and remains opaque to reflection, taunting our attempts to know. And most recently and most strikingly in this part of the tradition, one finds Derrida abandoning discursive analysis altogether, thinking of thinking as a futile enterprise that devolves into a collection of marginalia to a text—a text that he takes as a comic re-presentation of *savoir absolu*—open apparently to any interpretation whatever.

Whereas all of this supposedly grows out of a rejection of the presuppositions upon which the great systems were built, the new focus on indeterminacy that runs through the dialogue at this end of the contemporary spectrum is actually grounded in an obeisance to the oldest notions. It is the bias in favor of sameness, boundaries, and the determinate that leads to the kind of system being rejected, and instead of examining this fundamental presupposition, it seems to me that most if not all of the thinkers who have objected to the hegemony of the Absolute have focused simply upon its conclusions. Those conclusions are discarded because they leave no room for the place of difference, the unbounded and the indeterminate, and replaced with a speech that intends to recover the echoes of an unbounded Other. But this leads to the claim that the world is in some fundamental sense mysterious or unknowable only if we accept the notion that intelligibility is necessarily tied to boundaries and determinacy. As I have already said, I am sympathetic to the concerns that animate this movement. I entirely agree, for example, that the sweep of the Hegelian system illegitimately neglects the place of the individual, and does so precisely because of a misunderstanding of the relation between difference and negation. The labor of the negative, as Hegel understands it, is a labor grounded in its opposite, and one that ultimately gives itself over to the identity of identity and difference without allowing for the radical sense of difference that continues to evade the mediation of the Absolute Idea. On the other hand, we cannot afford to abandon ourselves to the negativity of an exclusive focus on difference, the unlimited, the indeterminate, if we are to be true to our own experience. As I shall show, the indeterminate dimensions of experience are ontologically bound to sameness, limitation and determinacy. Hence, it is just as dangerous to deny the place of the general principles, laws, and structures that are grounded in sameness as it is to abandon ourselves to the unrestricted hegemony of an Absolute. It may be that Hegel leaps too quickly away from the immediacy and indeterminacy of Being into the categorially bound schemata of Determinate Being, but there must be a place for the determinate dimensions of our experience in any account that purports to offer a reasonable description of it.

And a concern for the recovery of the determinate dimensions of experience leads to other end of the contemporary spectrum. Here, instead of an emphasis on the indeterminate, there has been a continuing commitment to the establishment of boundaries and definition, an enduring faith that the modern drive toward clarity and distinctness will finally issue in an account of the world unclouded by the ambiguous nature of our ordinary experience. And, the reservations of Hume and the rest notwithstanding, the core of the so-called analytical tradition has continued to assume that if we just examine things carefully enough, experiment extensively enough, we will finally arrive at such an understanding. Although the central view of this tradition still exerts enormous influence on Western thinking, particularly in the natural and social sciences, there has been growing concern, and that from within its own ranks, about some of its basic presuppositions. Questions raised by thinkers like Wittgenstein, Quine, and Sellars, and more recently by Goodman and Rorty, have led to serious debate about whether we can legitimately suppose that there is some objective reality against which our ideas and propositions can be measured. The whole notion of correspondence to such a reality as the fundamental test of the truth has been called into question, and along with it, the place of epistemology in philosophical reflection. While on this side of the tradition, there may not be the same sort of celebration of the indeterminate, there is nonetheless a developing position that seems to accept and even to endorse the notion that there is a certain indeterminacy about our experience that cannot be evaded no matter how cautiously we proceed.

On this view, it is not so much the place of difference and individuality in the Continental sense that is understood as the root of the problem, but the existence of a different kind of plurality. Given that the tradition has issued in any number of distinguishable and sometimes conflicting frameworks for explanation and description, Kuhn, Goodman, Rorty, and others, ask how we are to distinguish among them. If there is no ultimate or objective truth against which these various schemata can be judged, how are we to decide which is the right one? Must we abandon the notion that there is such a thing as the right one? Of course, there are various answers to these questions, but at the extremes of this end of the spectrum, there seems to be a growing consensus that, because there is no clear way of judging among competing theories, we must accept the fact that part of what has traditionally been understood as one of philosophy's primary tasks should simply be abandoned. Understanding epistemology as the attempt to identify the "right" theory, we are told that such a project must be abandoned along with the notion of correspondence as the fundamental criterion for truth.

The "indeterminacy" to be found in this sort of view also seems to arise from a continuing commitment to determinacy as a basic character of any intelligible account. We are presented with a plurality of determinate frameworks that are supposed to stand independent of one another. When it turns out to be impossible to establish the ascendency of any single framework, it is suggested that no such determination can be made, and that we should instead accept the notion that there exists an array of alternative frameworks, each suited in one fashion or another to its own context and procedures. Although these frameworks are bounded and defined when considered in themselves, the larger picture is one that lacks definition or determinacy just to the extent that the possibility of transcendent ontological criteria has been abandoned. The indeterminacy of this picture is importantly distinct from that typical of the Continental tradition mentioned previously, however, in that there appears to be no insistence that it arises out of the nature of Being itself, but should be understood as a function of our attempts to understand, or of the relation between Thought and Being. Still, it is an indeterminacy in experience, at least in reflective experience, that is represented as inevitable and as carrying significant consequences along with it, not least of which is the transformation of the philosophical project as already mentioned.

Now all of these views deserve much more careful treatment than I have time to give them here. I believe that important insights are to be gained from most if not all of them and shall take up a more direct consideration of them in the third book of this trilogy. The point in mentioning them now is to try to give the reader some sense of why I have undertaken the project of the present essay. It seems to me that we have not considered with sufficient care the nature of the crucial ontological principles and concepts that shape this current dialogue as they have shaped much of the tradition to which it responds. It may well be that understanding itself issues in a certain indeterminacy or uncovers such a dimension within being or both, but it is not for the reasons that either side of the "postmodern debate" has offered. There is no reason to abandon ourselves to the notion that the world is mysterious (in the sense of concealing itself from us) any more than there is to suppose that the character of knowing itself lies somehow beyond our reach. Both of these notions rest upon the more fundamental idea that intelligibility must be by definition determinate, and can be seen as functions of the quite reasonable suggestion that there are dimensions of our experience that are recalcitrantly indeterminate. I want to argue that the difference celebrated by one side of the spectrum, and the plurality insisted upon by the other, are both functions of the structure of determinacy itself, and of its necessary ontological relation to indeterminacy. It is quite legitimate to argue that we cannot neglect—much less eradicate—indeterminacy as a crucial and natural part of our experience, but this does not in the least mean that we must surrender ourselves to the idea that the world cannot be known, or that the task of philosophy is futile.

We must simply attend more carefully to the character of our own understanding, recognizing within it echoes of the nature of the world that we seek to know. Indeterminacy is as natural a part of the order of thought as it is of the order of being; and since at the deepest level of reflection, the line between thought and being is at most an artificial one, there is no point in trying to argue that the inevitable play between determinacy and indeterminacy is any more a function of the one than of the other. We must turn to a close investigation of the fundamental ontological structure of the relation between determinacy and indeterminacy if we are to understand how and why our attempts to know the world in an exclusively determinate manner have failed, beginning to see that far from signaling the "end of philosophy," this means only that it is time for another fundamental reassessment of our continuing attempt to know.

I believe that a misunderstanding of the relation between determinacy and indeterminacy has led to a pervasive misunderstanding of the logical structure of intelligibility itself that has infected the Western philosophical tradition from its inception. In neglecting the *ontological reciprocity* of the relation between the determinate and indeterminate dimensions of thought and being, we have consistently led ourselves astray. Throughout most of the tradition this mistake has emerged in the guise of a constant and unquestioning acceptance of the notion that all of our most basic paradigms for thought and being must have a determinate character. Although on the face of it there seems to be nothing either unnatural or unreasonable about this assumption, it turns out to be based upon a critical logical blunder.

It is not possible to separate the determinate dimensions of either immediate or reflective experience from their necessary relation to the indeterminate dimensions of experience without destroying the ontological underpinnings of the determinations that we seek to employ in the serious labor of understanding. Because no determinate principle, law, or category can be articulated independently of this more fundamental relation, a certain indeterminacy is a necessary byproduct of the very attempt to draw the world and our understanding of it into the determinate schemata we construct. This means neither that we should surrender ourselves to the notion that Being falls away from understanding into some ultimately ineffable abyss, nor that we should suppose that Thought must always despair of its consummation in a return to the concrete ground out of which it arises. We must bring ourselves to recognize that the very act of reflecting, which is itself a crucial part of the immediate experience of rational being, requires the reciprocal play of determinacy and indeterminacy in such a way as to undermine even the most refined and cautious attempt to capture our experience by means of sheerly determinate models of intelligibility.

The point is not—as many contemporary voices would have it—that the tradition has successfully brought to completion an examination of the determinate side of experience, and should now turn its attention to the indeterminate dimensions of experience. It is rather that in misunderstanding the relation between these two dimensions of thought and being, we have consistently misunderstood even those determinate dimensions of experience to which we have turned most of our attention. In supposing that the determinate dimensions of experience can be treated independently, we have deluded ourselves into aspiring to complete our speech about the world and frustrated ourselves at every turn by discovering that however complete our accounts become, something always seems to be left out.

To say that something is missing in our accounts, that the modern project of completing the speech has failed, is to say nothing that every serious thinker of the last century and a half hasn't already noted in one fashion or another. But in none of those thinkers have I found a satisfactory account of the *ontological ground* of this problem. It is this ground that I seek to expose in this book, and as a result, its primary focus will be a logical one. It is not my intention to trace the history of the various comments that have been made about "indeterminateness" and related concepts within the parameters of the tradition as it stands. In fact, because doing so would necessarily involve a consideration of arguments built upon the very presuppositions that I mean to call into question, I believe that the fundamental point that I want to make would in the end be obscured.

Moreover, since the mistake concerning the relation between determinacy and indeterminacy is made at the very beginning of the tradition, any useful reassessment of this relationship must be undertaken independently of the developed systems of thought to which a scholarly treatment of the issue would typically refer. Each of these positions actually amounts to the articulation of some particular set of determinately conceived presuppositions, principles, categories, and so on, and their distinctions from one another take on the same character. Whether one thinks in broad strokes, as, for example, considering the antagonism between the empiricists and the rationalists, or the ancients and the moderns, or in more particular terms by thinking of Aristotle's objections to Plato, or Kierkegaard's to Hegel, we have been too ready to suppose that someone must be right and that the fundamental task of philosophy is to find out who that is.

As I have already suggested, the contemporary philosophical landscape grows even wilder, because in addition to an assortment of thinkers representing each of the historical positions, there is a growing faction of serious thinkers who identify themselves specifically by despairing of being able to pick out any position whatever. What has been consistently neglected in all of this is the fundamental fact that *no* determinate position of any kind can be marked out without an intelligible other, and that as a result the character of the other *enters into* any given determinate system as a crucial ontological dimension of its own structure. Accepting this notion leads to a radical reassessment not only of the history of philosophy, but also of its future. But before any such reassessment can be fruitfully undertaken, I believe that the fundamental ontological point must be made as forcefully and independently as possible. Thus, I shall confine my comments about the tradition to a small number of foundational arguments (in Parmenides, Plato, and Descartes) that clearly expose what I take to be the mistaken bias in favor of determinacy that has shaped the tradition as a whole.

Before turning to that argument, I should like to make one final note about where the position that I shall be developing fits into the contemporary philosophical landscape. As I have suggested, I understand my view to fall somewhere between the extreme ends of the contemporary spectrum and in fact hope that it may in some measure lay open a logical path toward a reconciliation of those extremes. As such, it is a view that is aligned with and that draws upon the ideas of a growing number of thinkers who also seem to me to locate themselves toward the center of this spectrum. Although the scope and character of the argument of this book precludes any direct commentary on these positions, I want to acknowledge my debt to these teachers and colleagues at the outset. For some time now there has been a resurgence of systematic philosophy following on the work of Peirce, James, Whitehead, and others that, while recognizing the flaws of the modern quest for completeness, at the same time continues to assume that philosophy's basic task involves coming to grips with the fundamental questions that gave the tradition its original impetus. The work of Weiss, Hartshorne, Findlay, Buchler, Blanshard, their students and now their students' students, is leading to the establishment of a new tradition in systematic thinking determined to return to an investigation of those fundamental questions. However diverse the contributions of these thinkers may be, they are drawn together by a common commitment to a search for a better understanding of the world and to the belief that we are quite capable of reaching such an understanding.[5] Success in this undertaking requires now more than ever a reassessment of the basic ontological structures that shape our experience, and in the chapters that follow, I hope to make a contribution to this developing dialogue by rethinking one of the most fundamental of those structures, the relation between determinacy and indeterminacy.

---

5.   See, for example, *New Essays in Metaphysics*, ed. Robert C. Neville (Albany: State University of New York Press, 1987) which includes an earlier version of this chapter together with essays by a number of these thinkers.

CHAPTER 2

DETERMINATIONS, BOUNDARIES, AND DETERMINACY

Guildenstern: Yes, I'm very fond of boats myself. I like the way
they're— contained. You don't have to worry about which way to go,
or whether to go at all—the question doesn't arise, because you're on
a *boat*, aren't you?

Rosencrantz & Guildenstern Are Dead

I. INDETERMINACY AND BOUNDARIES

Glancing up over an earlier version of the preceding chapter, a former
teacher said, "I think I'm beginning to see your point, but you'll have to tell
me something more about what you mean by indeterminacy." I was more
struck than usual by the fact that I really had no clear response. At least, I
didn't have one of the sort that he wanted, or for that matter, of the sort that
I would have liked to provide. The notion of indeterminacy had already
come to figure so centrally in my thinking that I could scarcely make any
philosophical claim, whether talking to an introductory class or to philosoph-
ically sophisticated colleagues without making reference to it, and yet when
asked directly what I meant by it, I found that I was stuck. In one sense, this
is not surprising. Whatever it means, the term *indeterminacy* is presumably
one that does not give itself over to straightforward definition. If it did, we
should have to invent another word to refer to that which does not. On the
other hand, if *indeterminacy* is taken to refer merely to a lack of definition,
it is not clear that it has any place in serious philosophical reflection. Such
reflection has from the beginning developed not least as the search for definition, for some way, as we would typically say, of "making sense" out of
things. The assertion that there are some things that simply do not make
sense is one of the few assertions that is of no philosophical interest whatever. This is of course just the epistemic version of the Parmenidean insight

that introduced a self-conscious logic into our tradition. If you set up two choices, give one a wholly positive character and the other a wholly negative character, you find that there really is no choice. The wholly negative is not useful even as a logical place holder. It means nothing whether in respect to thinking or to being. This is not to say, however, that there is no point in thinking about the *relation* between the wholly positive and the wholly negative, because its peculiar character opens up a path toward an understanding of what I am more and more inclined to treat as the most fundamental of all logical relations, the relation between determinacy and indeterminacy. But more of this later when we return for a closer look at Parmenides and his earliest critic, Plato.

All of this passed through my mind as I tried to come up with some reasonable (and short) response to my teacher's question. Part of my problem, I suppose, was that I was looking for a short response. We have been talking about philosophy for almost twenty years and are accustomed to communicating in the kind of shorthand language that naturally develops in long-term friendships. Moreover, we had just been looking at some of each other's work, and wanted to get to a conversation about some specific issues that were only tangentially related to my broader interest in the character of indeterminacy. He was, at least for the moment, asking only for a clarification of terms. And as he is inclined to adopt a rather ahistorical position in conversations of this kind, he was not willing to tolerate the sort of references that I would typically use in other conversations with colleagues or students. I have often tried to get round this problem by tossing off references to Anaximander's apeiron, or Anselm's characterization of the nature of God, or Vico's corsi, and so on. But because none of these were acceptable in this context, I looked for examples in direct experience that might do as well. The things that came to mind were actually other questions. What does an oboe sound like? What color is the sea? What distinguishes one person, qua individual, from another?

In themselves, such questions obviously didn't provide a very helpful response, but they did provide a place from which to begin. What is interesting about them is that they are all questions that have answers, but whose answers have a curious sort of character. They seem at once to be limited and to defy limitation, to lie within boundaries of a sort, and yet to remain unbounded—at least in the sense that their boundaries are non-definite.[1]

The sound of an oboe is familiar to anyone acquainted with Western music of the last several centuries. Moreover, it is a sound so distinctive as to

---

1.   The sense in which the same might be said of natural language itself is related to this issue, but not directly to the point here. It is not to the shifting contours of ordinary language that I mean to draw attention, though it may be productive to take up such a consideration in time.

be easily identified even when heard in the midst of a wide variety of other contrasting and complementary sounds. Yet when one tries to describe its peculiar quality, none of the words that come to mind seem adequate to the task. One might be inclined to put this down to the range of sounds that the instrument makes, to the highly variable character of its tone. Played by a master, an oboe can sound reedy and plaintive at one moment, roundly rich and mellow at the next, and reach through all the colors and textures of sound between. No such description is particularly helpful though, inasmuch as one might use precisely the same language to describe other instruments—both similar, as, for example, a bassoon, and different, as, say, a violin—or for that matter a human voice. It might be possible to refine by expanding here, to distinguish the sound we are after by comparison and contrast with those others that might sometimes be described in similar terms but which nevertheless remain distinct. But one already knows before setting out on such elaborate descriptions that the result will be unsatisfactory; unsatisfactory, at least, if what we are after is something like a clear and distinct verbal representation of the oboe's sound. Still, however elusive such a representation may be, our knowledge of the sound remains firm and true. We *do* know what it sounds like and can demonstrate this in any number of ways.

Imagine someone who had never heard an oboe, but who was familiar with other Western instruments trying to get a sense of its sound by asking about its relation to this and that. Does it sound like a trumpet? Like a french horn? No to the first, occasionally to the second, we might say. (Odd, since they sometimes sound like each other.) Someone who knows what an oboe sounds like could presumably respond to any number of such questions correctly. The important point here is that such questions can also be answered incorrectly. An oboe does not sound like a trombone. Ever. Although the descriptions that we might offer of the sound are many and various, possibly forming an indefinitely large set, it is not at all true that any description would do: some descriptions are not only inappropriate, but quite simply wrong. This is part of what I meant previously by saying that the answer to the question is non-definitely bounded. If one can be wrong, there must be boundaries; if there are numerous ways of being right—and no absolute criteria for choosing among them in terms of something like "rightness"—the boundaries have a very curious character indeed.

At the moment, I am staying on an island off the west coast of Ireland, and as I write, I glance up from time to time at the constantly changing view from my window. To the north, there are the hills of Connemara, brooding mounds covered in mist on days like this one, lush and inviting on bright days when you can see buildings and fields and define a human presence. Galway City lies off to the east (by northeast) and the cliffs of Moher complete the semicircular bounds of Galway Bay to the southeast. At my back, to the south and west, looms the enormous presence of the sea. What color is the sea? Today, as a storm gathers force, it is steel gray, dark and ominous. Yesterday, it was green and blue, sparkling with welcome, one of those days when it seems natural to think of the sea as the mother of life itself. In fact, it is hard to think of a color that is not associated at some time or other with the sea. Even the red range burnishes it at sunset. But I suppose one is always conscious then of the colors as reflected and is much less inclined even in immediate experience to attribute the colors to the sea itself. The sophomore would like to inform us now that the sea really isn't any color at all; our confusion can be resolved by recognizing that it is the sort of physical structure that naturally reflects all colors. But this isn't really very helpful. Any child will tell you that the sea is blue—and not orange, say. What I mean is, if someone asks if the sea is orange, the answer is certainly no; if he asks whether it's blue, the answer is yes, more or less and sometimes. We usually connect the blue-green range with it, and the greens and blues that come to mind are of the sea alone, similar to but distinct from the greens and blues of the hills across the bay.

I remember walking along the cliffs at the back of the island a couple of years ago—for my money one of the most spectacular walks in Europe. These islands were formed when some gargantuan thrust lifted great sheets of carboniferous limestone up out of the sea, and it is impossible to walk along those cliffs, looking down to where the dynamic weight of the sea leans patiently against 300 feet of sheer rock wall, without thinking of sleeping giants. As a friend and I made our way along the cliff edge that day, we stopped now and then and (on hands and knees) looked down into the tiny coves and inlets that have been cut away from the rock wall. The waters there were an indescribably beautiful color, fascinating, almost hypnotic in their richness and depth. There are of course words that can be used to try to give the color to someone else, aquamarine, turquoise, and so on, but in the end one finds himself reaching for associations with other waters. The waters off the Amalfi Coast in southern Italy, for example, or surrounding the Cyclades in the Aegean have a similar sort of color on certain days, but it is only similar. We were actually heading toward Dun Dubchathair, (called the "Black Fort" in English), one of the ancient ring fortresses on the island. When we finally got there (much scrambling over stone walls is required), we found that the inlets on either side of the promontory enclosed by the fort sparkled with that same color but in an even more intense hue. As we began to explore the fort itself, we found some rocks on the west side splashed with bits of green and blue and white paint. It was one of those happy times when you experience a reassuring bond of fellow feeling with some anonymous other. We imagined him rushing back for paints and canvas, or possibly, having already lugged them with him over those walls, full of pleasure at having found a subject worth all the bother. But in either case, we were sure that he must have left disappointed. It just wasn't a color that paint could reproduce, though a very skillful artist might have been able to create an image that would call the original back to mind for someone familiar with it.

When we say of such a color that it is only to be found in the sea, it seems to me that we are tacitly referring to a color range of sealike tones within which this one finds a place. For we do after all know the color of the sea, however elusive it might seem to be when trying to reproduce it with words or paint. And here again, we are confronted by a perfectly familiar phenomenon that is certainly bounded by what it is not—orange, canary yellow, and so forth—but whose definition appears less and less distinct as our focus on it narrows toward precision. In fact, the very notion of precise definition seems peculiarly inappropriate in cases of this kind. It would be something like trying to give the feeling of those cliffs we walked along by informing someone about plate tectonics. At the same time, though, there are few things more clear in my mind than that color that Susan and I found in the sea. I find myself looking for it elsewhere and am quite certain that I would recognize it should I stumble on it again.

Should I pull up my socks and admit that I am deluding myself in this "certainty?" On what grounds could it make sense to do so? I hear myself in a classroom trying to get students to see what Descartes means. What is it that you are *really* certain of here? Isn't it that you are certain that you *think* that this or that is the case? And if that's true, the most that you are actually certain of is that your *thought* in some sense or other "is." Nonsense, they think—and occasionally say. And although they are quite wrong to think that the Cartesian turn is nonsense, they are also right to smell a rat. Two related but distinguishable notions of certainty are in play here, and it is unreasonable to use the logical standard appropriate to one as a criterion for judgment when considering the other. When I say that I am certain that I know that peculiar color, I do not at all mean to suggest that my certainty has the self-reflexively articulable character of the certainty that develops within closed or definitely bounded systems. It is not a systematic certainty. I cannot demonstrate my certainty by, for example, showing how the validity of this particular assertion is founded on its relation to other assertions and some series of logical bonds that tie them together. While it seems to make sense to think of the range of sealike colors as a system, it is not one of the sort that we typically call to mind as we do philosophy. It is a system in the sense of including a number of related elements, drawn together by similarities of the usual sort, but, at least considered from an experiential point of view, it is not a closed system, and as a result is not a framework capable of providing wholly determinate characters to its elements. This system constitutes a kind of enclosure since some things (colors of other sorts, tables, trees, geometry) are excluded from it, but while one can step outside the boundaries that mark the edges of the range of sea colors, there is no clear and precise way of identifying the boundary over which one has stepped. That there is a boundary remains undeniable, however, and I am more and more convinced that a better understanding of the relation between boundaries of this sort and those of the Cartesian sort will open a new kind of logical path.

The same question of boundaries (or the lack of them) arises quite naturally in considering the third question I mentioned earlier. "Persons," if we think about them from the point of view of ordinary experience, amount as much as anything to a kind of bounding of personal experience. Where do I begin and others leave off? The notion of an inside and an outside is so deeply ingrained in our usual contact with others that we are inclined to neglect it altogether until reflective questions about "selves" arise. Not long ago, when a friend and I were speculating on the motives of a mutual acquaintance who had acted in a way that seemed very much out of the way with respect to his usual behavior, we found ourselves saying (with resignation) that one never really knows the inside of anyone else. No matter how well we know even those closest to us, we learn very early on that it is impossible to predict the behavior of others with any certainty. This is partly true simply because we can never be completely aware of the effect that idiosyncratic concerns may be having on their reactions to otherwise ordinary situations. But even when you know someone's daily experience and general background closely enough to be aware of such concerns, if the circumstances are unusual enough, or the concerns deeply enough seated, it is quite possible—and not even all that unusual—to be utterly surprised by the responses and actions that one meets. I have in mind those times when a friend becomes furious, or is deeply hurt, or unaccountably pleased by some action of one's own. Some small gesture of friendship elicits overwhelming gratitude, some comment intended in jest provokes rage, some facial expression (misinterpreted) brings cascades of tears. I don't mean to suggest that these are daily experiences, of course, but just that they are familiar to all of us. When such things happen, or after they have happened and have been in one fashion or another resolved, we are sometimes moved to reflect on the tenuous character of our knowledge of others, and as I've been saying, even of those others who are closest to us. Such reflections can yield, in fact, some of life's loneliest moments, moments when we feel suddenly apart, separate, much less sure of those "bonds of fellow feeling" that we are accustomed to rely on in both ordinary and reflective experience.

Still, however concrete the sense of an impenetrable "inside" to the other may be, trying to define and understand that interior dimension of the other often seems to lead us away from rather than toward our direct experience of it. No sooner are you convinced that you are confronted by a being whose self-identity so returns on itself as to form something ineluctably *other* than the general descriptions that we typically use of others (and of ourselves) appear to call this conviction into question. I try to think about what might possibly explain the behavior of my friend and immediately find myself drawing what I took to be atypical behavior into some larger pattern of behavior within which I hope to begin to understand it. What could make *me* act like that? When do other people act this way? What might I have overlooked that could explain the surprise that I felt on meeting this response from him? And ordinarily, it is relatively easy to find some possible or even likely explanation. Even if it takes some imagination, some frame or other will recommend itself, and what is often most surprising in such cases is that it can be used by the person in question to explain behavior that he himself may find equally mystifying. Most of these descriptions stand in direct conflict with the idea that there are any significant personal boundaries since they all seem to refer to ways in which the person is similar to what he is not. From the most general to the most particular, our descriptive language depends on mediation, that is, on frameworks drawn within practical and reflective experience that are constructed in the first place out of a focus on samenesses or at least similarities. As I shall argue in the next chapter, the logic of sameness *requires* an intelligible notion of otherness, and I mean to note here simply that the reverse is equally true. As soon as we try to make sense out of the other qua other, the notion of sameness intrudes, and becomes a crucial logical concept for our reflection.

But what is left out of the picture is just the thing that we were originally trying to illuminate. We are so accustomed to damping the effect of a confrontation with otherness in this way that we forget that it was the *fact* of otherness that we were trying to make sense of in the first place. And although the construction of explanatory frames is a very efficient stop-gap measure in practical terms, it is ultimately unsatisfactory both practically and theoretically. Practically, because people who use this sort of thinking as a way of interpreting their own behavior may fall into the trap of surrendering personal responsibility and thereby chipping away at the very thing that they seek to understand. Theoretically, because instead of producing the description of otherness that we sought, we end in convincing ourselves that it was just an illusion. The boundaries between the private and the public begin to fall away—and with them, the palpable otherness of the original confrontation—at the very moment that we begin to define them.

Hence "clarification" in this case has a curiously destructive character; we delude ourselves into thinking that we have solved problems that will in fact continue to resist any "solution" of this sort. But more of this later. For the moment, the point I mean to emphasize is really quite straightforward— at least, in this context. What is interesting here is the fact of the surprise, not the fact that there are various ways of using that surprise as a starting point that will lead down familiar reflective paths. The surprise, taken as a brute fact of experience, is one of those things that makes us aware of others as others. And if we go on to focus simply on that sense of otherness, we can draw it into our own experience as a kind of external instance of the feeling that all of us have of an interior. We can make sense out of the others' behavior as a sign that points to boundaries of the sort that we are often conscious of in thinking of our own relations to them. (I remember the time that she was puzzled by my reaction to . . . And where, equally as puzzled, I was given a sense of myself as both the cause of the puzzlement and one puzzled.) In fact, it may be here that one finds the seat of the indeterminacy that expresses itself in the vague character of the boundaries that define a person as this rather than that one. There is a tension that no one else is ever privy to between the thinker as subject and object. We are made aware that the other person must have an "inside," and correspondingly that we have "outsides," and that, however difficult they may be to articulate, the boundaries between the two are as real as any part of our experience.

II. BOUNDARIES IN DIRECT EXPERIENCE

I think again of the scene before me. This island, like much of Ireland, is checkered with stone walls dividing what in many cases seem to be uselessly small bits of land from one another. The island is fraught with boundaries, and is itself more obviously bounded than the land masses on which most of us live and work. Galway Bay lies before me, stretching around my ordinary field of vision, but in such a way that I am aware likewise of its boundaries. And then behind me, there is the sea. The walled fields, the island, the bay, the sea, are each of them bounded in some sense of the term, but none of them in quite the same way.

For one thing, the artificial boundaries formed by the stone walls are much more definite than any of the others. They maintain a constant character from year to year, usually changing only as the result of actions as deliberate as those that originally formed them. The other boundaries are all much less clear. The shape of the island, like that of any island, is in a state of continual change. The wind and the sea change its outlines from year to year; in the season of storms, from day to day. Large pieces of the cliff edge plummet into the sea periodically, erasing familiar paths, sometimes significantly altering the whole aspect of a favorite spot. On the protected northeasterly side, there are beaches whose contour and definition change as soon as one marks them out. The island is bounded all right—one knows, for example, what it means to be on or off it—but its bounds are not really much like their abstract image as represented, say, by the black lines on the map in my bedroom.

Galway Bay is even more difficult to define. There it lies before me, but where the bay stops and the sea begins is even less clear than where the beach begins and ends. The age-old fascination with the water is no doubt partially a function of this curious play between definition and formlessness. Our attempts to capture and tame the sea by thinking of it as made up out of manageable bits and pieces are, if not altogether futile, certainly dubious from the start. And when our attention turns to the sea as a whole, the task seems hopeless. From one perspective, its boundaries are fairly clear. I saw its edges as I took off from New York and landed at Shannon a few days ago. But it was hard to take those images seriously as, my feet on the ground again, I gazed out at the somber and swelling presence of the Atlantic from the island's formidable western cliffs. At the highest point there, one is surrounded by Dun Aenghus, another of the ancient ring fortresses, and experiences much the same sense of being at the westernmost edge of the world that must have awed the fort's builders. Only mythical lands lie out there in the immeasurable beyond. On a misty day, it's much easier to believe in Tir na Nog than in the streets and shops of Reykjavik.

Now as boundaries, the walls seem more definite than the others. That is true not only as a physical fact, but likewise because they have an immediately recognizable human import. We know what walls are for, how they are built, when and why they disappear. Interestingly, with these walls at least, one finds a curious mixture of strength and weakness. They are able to withstand terrific gusts of wind and rain, but crumble into heaps of rubble if one leans on them carelessly. The bits of land that they mark out have an equally human significance, as one imagines some father cutting up his tiny piece of land and parceling it out to too many children. Here we have boundaries of the most fundamentally human sort. This is mine: Keep Out. But the very fact of their deliberate construction, while it lends them a definite character at any given moment, likewise seems to deprive them of one when we think about them from a reflective distance. A thing constructed by one person can be destroyed by another. We needn't wait with poor Ozymandias for the gentle erosion of the ages; sufficient force or persuasion can do away with these walls in a moment. The little kingdom disintegrates into nothing much more quickly than it was built. And conscious of this, we see these boundaries as extremely tenuous ones. The bits of land can easily merge into the larger whole from which they were carved in the first place, and the immediate significance of the walls, the meaning that they seem to have at this moment or that, dissolves just as easily.

The boundaries of the island, at first seemingly less definite, turn out to be firmer on reflection. Here there is no deliberation, no creature of will that is susceptible to some other will. The island is what it is, however much it may be the case that its borders shift from time to time. And it has been what it is for a very long time. (Those forts that keep coming to mind may be as much as 5,000 years old.) Moreover, its dimensions are such that there are points where one can stand and see right round the place. Upon doing so, one sees a "place" that is importantly different from the parcels of land, since the seeing doesn't seem to have anything much to do with the definition of the thing seen. The island, one thinks to himself, would have boundaries whether I was conscious of them or not, and is certainly in this sense distinguishable from the islanders' plots. Of course, one no sooner thinks such a thing than the rationalistic tradition calls itself to mind, with the reminder that the boundaries of the island do indeed have to do with consciousness, inasmuch as there is no very good reason to suppose that either the island or the sea much cares where it stops or starts. And since trying to adopt an unconscious point of view seems a rather fruitless enterprise, . . .

But putting such reflections aside for the moment, we can perhaps agree that the boundaries of the island, far from depending on this or that individual, do not even seem to depend on any age of humankind. Several of those ages have left their marks on the island, from the ring fortresses to the monastic settlements, from the Cromwellian barracks to the power plant, and the island was here through all of them, a place—if not an altogether hospitable one—to be inhabited. Well, then, what of the island's boundaries? Here, *on* and *off* seem to be more natural terms than, say, *inside* and *outside*, but the line that divides them is, as I have said, at once more concrete and less clear than the lines of the walls. The lines of the map may be rather like those of the walls, but the actual shorelines are not. They are clear only from a distance, and contrary to what we (as moderns) typically expect in reflective experience, become vaguer and ultimately disappear altogether as we approach them. At least, they disappear if what we are searching for is the original of the map's image, supposing that such an original would be a more clearly defined line. The shoreline is still there, immediately and certainly distinct from the sea, but it does not in itself provide us with the ground of the distinction between being "on" or "off" the island. Am I off the island when I put one foot in the water? Both feet? When I swim out ten yards at high tide? One hundred yards at low tide?

If there isn't a line that will do as a boundary, what about some distinct character that the island has? Perhaps what we mean when we say that the island is bounded is that it has some quality or nature that distinguishes it. It is solid whereas the sea is liquid, and hence bounded by a quality that applies to it but not to the sea. This of course solves one problem only by presenting another. We can distinguish this island from its surrounding waters in this way, but not from, for example, the other two islands that form the Aran group. And the same will obviously hold for any of the many more specific characteristics that we might settle on as defining characters. If they don't apply to the other two islands of this group, they will certainly apply to some island or other. If we grow still more specific in our thinking, and seek individuation by means of particular things that are to be found on this island and no other, this fort, this church, that village, we would actually meet with no greater success, and would soon seem to be departing from our original task in any case. After all, the question we were asking was a fairly simple one, and if the answer becomes turned and twisted too far from the straightforward tone of the original question, there is good reason to think that we are on the wrong track. Should we find ourselves trying to bound the island either by mentioning that Dun Aenghus stands on its highest point, or, worse still, by positioning it as uniquely occupying a spatiotemporal position in some inertial framework, the boundaries that we were after will remain out of reach, receding as the concrete almost invariably does from the playgrounds of abstraction. (Dun Aenghus is concrete enough, to be sure, but not when used as a defining characterstic, and the inertial frame is hopelessly abstract from the start.) The more we try to demonstrate that the island is determinate by pointing to the fact that it has boundaries, the less determinate it seems to be.

We are inclined to assume that the determinacy of things comes from some a priori definition that picks them out of the field of our experience willy-nilly, but laying hands on that definition turns out, even in relatively simple cases, to be a much more complicated project than ordinary experience leads us to suppose. In ordinary experience, of course, things are already defined by the context within which one is operating, and there is rarely any reason to look for the logical basis of their definition. The potatoes in the shop are there to be bought and eaten, not thought about. Nor is their ontological distinction from the tomatoes something that gives us much reason for pause while we are planning dinner.

I am scouting the possibility that it is the act of making-determinate that constitutes the boundaries, not the boundaries that make such acts possible. This is, so far, scarcely a startling suggestion. Its strengths and weaknesses have been thoroughly examined and tested by the rationalistic side of the tradition, and dealt with at least in passing by the empirical side that takes as its starting point a logical position three or four giant steps beyond the problem we are considering. What I think we have not attended to with sufficient care is the play between determinacy and indeterminacy that appears in the act of making-determinate, in the establishment of boundaries of the various sorts that I have been calling to mind. These boundaries are typically supposed to exist "out there," firmly separating something from what it is not, and in most circumstances separating one apparently determinate object from another equally determinate object, as in the case of the parcels of land distinguished one from the other, or the island as distinct from the sea in which it lies. But if the boundaries turn out to be much harder to define than ordinary experience leads us to believe, the determinacy we attributed to the objects that these rather ephemeral and elusive boundaries supposedly work to separate is also called into question. The concrete character we usually attribute to determinacy starts to tremble somewhat.

It may have seemed at first that, in considering things like the sound of an oboe, the color of the sea, distinguishing one person from another, I was focusing on peculiarly indeterminate moments or shapes of experience. But even when we start with rock walls, a certain indeterminacy appears as soon as we move only a bit beneath the surface of unreflective phenomenal description. In this preliminary thinking about boundaries—I shall return to the notion later on in other contexts—I started with the walls intentionally. It might be possible to dismiss the indeterminacy of the sound or the color as something that has to do with the vagaries of sense perception, but if it turns out that the same thing is true of stone walls, there is perhaps a more obvious reason for concern. The definition of the bits of land seems to me no more secure—in fact, in some ways, less—than that of the sound and the color. Or, to put the point in terms of the other immediate boundaries that play a role in the scene from my window, they are no more secure than the boundaries that mark the inside and outside of Galway Bay. The bounds of the bay may be more obviously open to question when considered phenomenally, but their character is really no more tenuous than that of the boundaries that palpably divide the land.

Nor does putting this down to the effect of human invention get us very far. It is not that humanly constructed boundaries are somehow less real or less definite than nonhuman ones, but rather that all the boundaries of our experience, in marking out one thing as opposed to another, depend on a kind of otherness that as we shall see does not itself fall within the frameworks that it makes possible. I think that we find in the elusive character of these boundaries an instance in direct experience of the necessary role of indeterminacy in theoretical experience. When we stand back from an uncritical acceptance of the determinacy of things to seek after the ground of determinacy itself, we find that something else is required. Determinacy does not seem able to stand on its own; its logical ground is at least as slippery as that of the boundaries I have been considering.

In most contexts it is possible to allow the determination of things to be governed by the determination of other things—as, say, a variety of fruit in a bowl: this sort of thing is an apple, as distinct from that, which is an orange. And, thinking again in terms of ordinary experience, it seems reasonable to treat determination of this sort as grounds for thinking that the world as a whole is basically determinate in structure. But I intend to show that the formation of determinate contexts of any sort whatever, and equally of the particular determinations that they generate, requires a concept of indeterminacy (though it is an odd "concept" certainly) that remains logically distinct from and is not reducible to the concept of determinacy. I am aware that there is something rather strange about treating determinacy, let alone indeterminacy, as a "concept" inasmuch as it is usually taken to be that on which the intelligibility of concepts depends, but at this stage of my scouting expedition, I should prefer to ask the reader's indulgence than to invent some new word.

III. DETERMINACY I

Before turning to a discussion of the play of otherness in the act of making determinate, it might be well to think at least briefly about the relatively comfortable notion of determinacy. When my teacher asked me about indeterminacy, he was presumably doing so because he assumed that we both understood what we meant by determinacy, and that it was in my claims about the indeterminate dimensions of experience that I might have something new to say. And this is a perfectly reasonable assumption for philosophers to make. Reflective discourse of any sort depends on stable conceptual determinations, and while we might in this context or that call some particular determination into question, the idea that there are determinations of some sort is as important to our disagreements as it is to our agreements. One has to start somewhere, and the place typically chosen by philosophers is defined by determinate structures. Moreover, the practical contexts from which reflective discourse emerges depend equally on a recognition of determinations. If we think of practice in terms of problem solving, say, it becomes immediately obvious that we would be unable to so much as formulate problems to ourselves, let alone uncover successful solutions, without having first separated the stream of our experience into manageable segments.

   Consider the most basic and concrete of the practical problems that confront us: providing ourselves with sufficient food, shelter, and clothing to survive. Long before we maneuver ourselves into the position of drawing fine distinctions between living and living well (in the Socratic sense), we are forced by the exigencies of practical experience to define our lives by distinguishing various immediate and long-term needs, and by the methods and means that we invent to fulfill them. We apportion our time and energy in accord with these ends and means, naturally dividing and categorizing experience as we proceed. Life itself, at the most basic level, takes on a determinate character as we identify needs and look around us in the world for ways of satisfying them. The world in which we carry out this activity takes on an equally determinate character then, sorting itself out before us into what is useful and what is not. Some things are good to eat, some are not, some things can be woven into cloth, others can't. And our practical success expands and develops as we refine those primitive distinctions, constructing increasingly complex frameworks of classification, more efficient ways of dividing labor, and so on.

Nor is it only the concrete objects around us that give themselves over quite naturally to these classifications. Abstract dimensions of immediate experience likewise enter into the world of practical problems and solutions as things that can be handled best when treated as determinately structured. I have in mind notions like space and time, and their ordinary shapes in direct experience. Beginning with fundamental dividing lines between here and there, now and then, the growing complexity of practical needs and methods naturally issues in complicated schemes of spatial and temporal measurement. How much space must be enclosed to provide a liveable shelter, how much land cleared to produce the desired quantity of grain, and so forth. More interestingly, questions concerning the relation of the past to the future arise as we recognize the need to develop accurate methods of prediction to ensure long-term survival and to guard as securely as possible against the various contingencies that have interrupted the flow of life in the past. And it's only a hop, skip, and a jump to a consideration of the relation between motion and rest as equally fundamental aspects of our direct experience or at least as concepts a better understanding of which can further our progress toward various ends.

A certain kind of determinacy appears to be wedded to our most rudimentary intercourse with the world. Dividing our experience into thises or thats and proceeding with the task of classification is as natural to us as breathing. In fact, it is an activity without which we would not breathe for long. It is not surprising, then, that when we do finally provide ourselves with sufficient time to support the luxury of abstract reflection, our first inclination is to follow the same path, seeking some set of similarly determinate logical forms that can function as theoretical analogues to the practical determinations of customary experience. But some difficulties arise. Where in practical experience, determinacy looms large as a sort of sine qua non, it presents problems almost immediately for abstract reflection. Here it is equally crucial of course, but no matter where we begin, its own character, something that we might think of as the "determinacy of determinacy," throws a wrench into the works.

Say we start off as the Milesians did, searching for an utterly fundamental physical structure, some something out of which everything else is made. Water appears immediately as a reasonable possibility. We can only speculate about Thales' reasons for choosing it, but some fairly noteworthy ones come readily to mind. It appears as a liquid, solid, and a gas in common experience. Perhaps more importantly, it seems to be *inside* things, especially if we assume that he is using *water* as a generic term for liquids of various sorts; for example, blood, sap, semen, magma. What lives cannot do without it, both in the direct physical sense and (particularly for someone who lives by the sea) in the more complex social and political senses where it is crucial for travel, commerce, education, and so forth. Given all of this—and the expanded list that just a bit more thought could produce—suppose we consider that we have found the most fundamental of elements and proceed to develop an argument that everything is made out of water. The next move would clearly be an attempt to reconcile its apparent character with those of other almost equally fundamental things, for example, earth, air, and fire. Earth and air present no real problem, inasmuch as they can be accounted for with the move to a slightly more general reading of the term *water*—the solid can become liquid, in fact may appear to have come from the liquid in the first place in a volcanic region; the liquid can produce a gas—but fire cannot be accounted for quite so easily. If we are still trying to reason from phenomenal or practical experience, fire seems to destroy and to be destroyed by water, presenting itself as an opposite. Even if we reform the meaning of fire by generalizing it to "heat," there are significant difficulties. How or whether Thales got round these problems we don't know, but it seems quite possible that it was a consideration of such a problem that lead Anaximander to propose a different kind of fundamental term altogether, the *apeiron*. But more of that in a moment. First, we might gain some insights by thinking about some of the problems that present themselves in the simpler scheme suggested by Thales.

As soon as we try to construct a reflective schema that is constituted by one or more determinations, we find ourselves having to come to terms with the character of determinacy itself. Even if we posit only a single fundamental determination as Thales did, direct experience demands distinctions within the framework of our logical account that will correspond to the differentiation of the phenomenal world. So that if we choose water as a fundamental term, arguing that it can stand as such by itself, it is nonetheless natural to begin to make distinctions within its nature in terms of aspects, properties, qualities, and so on. (Water qua solid, liquid, gas; water qua medium for the growth of food; water qua means of transportation.) What distinguishes these aspects from one another? The answer cannot be "water." All the aspects and properties are watery. Nor does it suffice to say that they just *are* distinct. The whole point of our exercise is to develop a *logical* account, one that answers questions, not one that begs them. And this means that we are obliged to provide a reasonable answer to the question of how things are different from one another while at the same time participating in a coherent whole.

If (in this scheme) water accounts for sameness, what accounts for difference? We start with water, find that it presents itself as an attractive starting place indeed, but also find that to allow our account to expand, widening sufficiently to embrace the apparent specificity of direct experience, a logical notion that is not identical with water is required. Water appeared attractive in the first place because of its ability to maintain a single identity while manifesting that identity in distinguishable forms. In fact it may not be going too far to say that it is primarily as a ground for such distinctions that water actually recommends itself. Or, in any case, its inherent plurality is at least as important as its logical role in providing a foundation for sameness. If we are to settle on a single term as the foundation for a logical account, it must be one that can contribute determinacy to the account not only in the sense of maintaining a consistent self-identity, but also in the sense of allowing for differentiation within that identity. In other words, determinacy cannot be thought of as identical with the first term, because then there would be no logical place for any other meaningful term of any kind. If, in the case of our primitive scheme, water and determinacy are taken to be indistinguishable, then obviously there can be nothing but water. And that means *nothing*. There could be no meaningful way of distinguishing among different aspects or properties of water any more than there would be a way of distinguishing water from anything else.

The logical character of determinacy must remain distinct from the first term, no matter what term is chosen. This is equally true when the first term has a wholly abstract character as, say, "being" has. When Aristotle criticizes the Milesians (and others) in the first book of the Metaphysics[2] for neglecting the principle of difference, and assumes that this results from their inclination to focus exclusively on material causes, he is right in one sense and wrong in another—to use an Aristotelian qualification. He is right to point out that some direct account of difference is required, and wrong to suppose that it can be supplied by merely multiplying the kinds of causes. However concrete or abstract the framework, the same difficulty will arise since there will always be the same play between sameness and difference. One cannot simply insist on a fundamental plurality, since unless the logical groundwork for a principle of difference is laid at the beginning of the account, the plurality—in Aristotle's case, multiple causes—will ultimately resolve itself into a univocal first term that cannot (by itself) support differentiation. If, as in Aristotle's account, sameness is given pride of place, and difference treated as derivative, the distinctions within the framework will ultimately collapse into a univocal and monolithic first term from which no other can be legitimately derived.[3]

The determinacy needed to flesh out our account cannot be provided by the self-identical character of a single term. While there is a certain determinacy included in the concept of self-identity, that is not the same as saying that the determinacy of the concept is contributed by the term that is being treated as self-identical. In the account I have been using as an

---

2.   *Metaphysics*, 988b23ff.
3.   Ibid., 1017b10ff.

example, this means that water and determinacy remain distinct, since if water were taken to coincide logically with determination per se, we would find ourselves trying to begin with a curious and logically useless abstraction. That is, if determinacy is equated with the first term, so that the first term becomes something like determinacy itself, no further speech is possible. It follows that determinacy would have a fundamentally indeterminate character, as something devoid of determinate content, and appear as logically barren as a boundary drawn around nothing.[4] But more than that, we need not only a sense of determinacy that can make sense of considering the first term, here, water, self-identical, but require equally a sense of determinacy that allows for the differentiations within the character of the first term without which an elaboration of the framework would be restricted to the mere assertion of the existence of water—which is in this case the existence of a univocal being whose fundamental character is watery. In other words, we will also require a sense of determinacy that enters into the internal structure of water and allows for the separation and distinction of forms, properties, and so on.

IV. INTERLUDE

In the introduction to the *Encyclopedia*, Hegel says that "to speak of a beginning of philosophy has a meaning only in relation to a person who proposes to commence the study, and not in relation to the science as a science."[5] I have commented elsewhere, and not very sympathetically, on Hegel's understanding of the relation of the beginning to the end in philosophical speculation.[6] But here, in making this comment after having argued that there is a fundamental unity to the philosophical enterprise, that the systems and theories that compose the tradition are in some sense all of a piece, I think that he is quite right. Put aside for the moment what Hegel means by *science*, and the imposition of his own view that that entails, and his comment has the ring of a fundamental truth. There is no single beginning to philosophy, for everyone who takes up the task of serious thought offers a new beginning; sometimes articulated in familiar terms, sometimes in strange and new ones. But there is at the same time a common theme that unites these beginnings, a single drive toward the truth that breathes life

---

4. This is the seat of the problem that Parmenides confronts and of the Hegelian conflation of Being and Nothing in the *Logic*, a problem that will be treated more fully in the next chapter.

5. G. W. F. Hegel, *The Encyclopedia of the Philosophical Sciences*, trans. William Wallace (Oxford: Oxford University Press, 1959), p. 28.

6. *Individuals and Individuality*, see esp. Ch. 4.

into the ideas that emanate from them. And there are also patterns of thought to be discerned in the development of those ideas that lend substance to the notion of some universal logic that makes it possible to look from one beginning to another, seeking fundamental logical stages in the development of thought itself.

In trying to imagine the world of the Milesians, thinking through the basic problems as they presented themselves to them, I do not suppose that we might uncover some different truth by returning to a simpler world, or that there is some lost understanding that might be recovered by reconsidering the possibility that the world is constituted by water and fire and so on. I am interested in thinking about the ways that they found of dealing with the same logical problems that confront anyone trying to make sense out of things. It doesn't really matter whether one starts with water and fire, or with the laws of thermodynamics; some of the basic logical issues that arise will be much the same. Just as the problem of the one and the many, the apparently irreconcilable contrast between sameness and difference must have frustrated them, so it frustrates us. One can imagine arguments between Thales and Anaximander not unlike those between, say, Einstein and Heisenberg, and on one level at least, there would be no important distinction. At the logical level, things have remained much the same. Our knowledge of the world is in one sense vastly more elaborate and sophisticated, in another, equally naive. For it continues to be as naive now as it was then to suppose that it is possible to successfully confine the many within the boundaries of the one by reducing difference to sameness, and it is equally naive to suppose that this means we cannot understand the world that we confront, construct and animate. It merely means that it is not possible to give a wholly determinate account of something that includes indeterminate aspects and dimensions.

Nonetheless, there is something to be learned by examining the ways that others have tried to do so. Moreover, while every thinker may be starting a new project, beginning again, it is still true that we are part of a common tradition, and that from that perspective, the beginning represented by the Presocratics is unique and importantly so. It is not only their beginning, but ours. And the ways that they found of dealing with the basic logical puzzles—however incomplete our knowledge of them—have influenced our thinking through the impact that they had on the thought of Plato and Aristotle. Although I do not intend to turn to the essentially scholarly task of examining references, matching up phrases, decodifying the often cryptic remains of what must have been a rich body of thought, I do want to trace in broad outline those influences as it seems they have continued to restrict our models of intelligibility. We may eschew this particular set of determinations or that, but seem always to replace them with other determinations whose character as determinations, and more importantly, whose *relations* to one another remain unchanged. Hence, it is not the particular efficacy of, for example, water as a primary term that should interest us, but the way that it is introduced into a logical framework as a first term, and its relations to the other terms that are gradually added to that framework to fill in the gaps.

It seems reasonable to suppose that the Milesians were what we would call natural scientists or, from the perspective of the philosophical tradition, materialists. However, it is too easy, having said that, to neglect the fact that materialism—in any of its forms—is an abstract conceptual framework. Conjuring up concrete terms as parts of the framework often has the effect of tricking us into thinking that we are dealing with something like the particulars of direct experience—much as the contemporary grade school student begins to suppose that molecules really are miniature versions of the styrofoam balls and sticks that the teacher holds in the front of the classroom. And, to be sure, the committed materialist does mean to argue that the stuff of the world has a basic character analogous to that of the objects at one's feet. Nonetheless, when this or that is identified as the basic stuff, it is always finally an abstraction that confronts us, not a rock. And it must be. For materialists must follow the logical path to the universal just as rationalists do, however much more assiduously they may try to cover their tracks. As soon as the claim that *everything* is made of this or that appears, we have removed ourselves from the particulars of experience and found a new footing in the universal concepts of logical schemata.

What is interesting about the various schemata apparently developed by the Milesians is not so much their respective successes as their failures. Why was it necessary to move beyond Thales' simple and logically elegant attempt to claim that everything is made out of a single substance? It may be that in considering some possible answers to that question, we can learn something more about the logical character of determinacy.

V. DETERMINACY II

Of the "primary elements," only fire stands apart from water with an insistent identity of its own. Far from falling neatly into an overarching watery scheme of things, it not only differentiates itself, but seems recalcitrantly opposed to the unifying sweep of such a scheme. Now, the first stage of our reflection has shown us that some ground for determination is required to articulate a scheme that can take account of the ordinary differences within experience and avoid the logical problem of depriving our first term of determinacy by identifying it with determinacy. Perhaps it is in the relation between water and fire that such a ground can be located.

Suppose we begin by thinking in physical terms again. What is it that physically distinguishes the three forms of water from one another? Heat, of course. The differences within sameness that made us posit water as a first term in the account actually depend for their distinct identities on the one element that doesn't give itself over to the embrace of the scheme we are trying to articulate. Far from destroying the systematic coherence of the account that is unfolding, fire, taken as a second term, may well enhance and augment its development. For it seems to provide at least some room for the differentiation without which the first term collapses into itself—into a logically barren identification of determinacy and indeterminacy—rather than issuing in the further determinations that will make the schema viable.

The question now is whether this means that fire can introduce the needed determinacy into our relatively primitive scheme of things. It is tempting at first to make a mistake similar to that of assuming that water carries along with it not only its own determinacy, but the ability to determine the other parts of the scheme. That is, we might imagine that in fire we have found the determinacy or the potential to make determinate the other shapes of the developing account. But what held true for water holds equally for fire. It can no more determine itself—in the sense of positing itself as equivalent to determinacy—than water can. In the context of this account at least, its determinacy seems to be a function of its relation to water; it is in the opposition between the two that the potential for their respective determination and for further determinations is located. Is it opposition then? Since the opposition between fire and water seems to provide a ground for determinacy in this scheme, couldn't we reasonably suggest that opposition itself be added as another term, albeit a term of a rather different sort, to water and fire to fill out an originative triad that would provide not only specific ground-level determinations, but also a seat for determinacy itself?

There is nothing inherently unreasonable about such a suggestion, but new problems begin to emerge. For one thing, the relation between fire and water, while it can be described as a kind of opposition, is a curious sort of opposition. It is not, for example, the same as what might be treated as opposition per se, logical contradiction. Unless we entirely separate the meanings of water and fire from their senses in direct experience—something we would do at the cost of similarly separating this kind of account from the experience that it was originally initiated to comprehend—they cannot be understood as logical opposites. This is partly true just because the terms *water* and *not-fire* are not coextensive. But more importantly, and again in relation to the development of our schema, fire (qua heat) actually *enters into* the constitution of water to the extent that water is a useful term in our system. Fire may be posited as something external to water and as giving water in this sense its determination as a discrete term in the system. But it also functions as that which makes the internal differentiation of water possible, and as such seems to penetrate the boundaries that it participates in constructing.

Or, the opposition between water and fire has the reciprocal effect of making each term determinate in its own right, but the opposition, when considered in terms not merely logical, that is, when seen also from the phenomenal or practical ground from which we began, turns out to be much more complicated than the relation that might be expressed symbolically with a tilde. In fact, thinking along these lines, imagining that we can strip the relation of its ambiguity by means of the reflective distancing peculiar to analytical logic, we destroy even what I called earlier the "external" determinacy contributed to the two terms by their opposition. Thinking of water as not-fire, in other words, doesn't really convey any of the concrete content of the phenomenon with which we began, or in any case, offers only a very pale image of the concrete character that we need if we are to build our system on firm ground. We are really after a way of identifying what it is in particular about water that separates it from fire, since we ultimately want to use whatever it is that water is in itself as a ground for the further determinations that will give our scheme its explanatory and/or descriptive efficacy. The same thing holds for fire. If we try to define it merely as not-water, the interesting if discursively elusive play between fire as internal and external to the nature of water dries up into a barren logical construct, into something like determinacy per se.

Some richer sense of opposition is called for. Or, it would be better to say that some richer understanding of the relation between water and fire seems essential to moving forward with the scheme. Opposition, after all, seems to represent only one dimension of the relationship, since as I suggested previously, a certain reciprocity is also involved in the logical play between *water* and *fire* considered as primary terms in a logical schema. In their opposition, they give rise to a reciprocal determination. Although such determination is not sufficient to account for anything like the concrete identities of the phenomena that we started with, it is attached at least to the generically broadened notions that they quickly become as they are introduced into a reflective scheme.

Water taken as a general term for the liquids that occupy a crucial and pervasive place in ordinary experience, and *fire* taken as a general term for heat in various degrees, interact significantly with one another in phenomenal experience. If the notion of the liquid is to be useful at all as a fundamental physical ground, the various appearances that are distinct from its most direct phenomenal form have to be held apart by something or other, and *heat* can be used as a name for the phenomenon that seems to hold them apart. Likewise, because we need some standard in terms of which to identify the varying degrees of heat that make the growth of the account possible, water can act reciprocally to give us a firmer grasp on heat (*heat* defined in terms of the various states of a liquid substance as it moves through the range of physical forms). The two play against each other in a fashion that is neither wholly determinate nor wholly indeterminate since each seems to enter into the phenomenal determination of the other, crossing the boundary that might seem quite firm if we were to attend to their relation only in terms of opposition.

Similarly, if we step back from the phenomenal relation to a consideration of the character of the play between the two terms now taken as abstract logical terms in a reflective framework, the relation seems again to refuse any simple logical definition. The terms are fairly straightforwardly distinguished from one another in terms of the most ordinary sense of opposition, but as we have seen, a kind of reciprocity enters the picture in such a way as to blur the edges of what would otherwise be reducible to a neat logical contrariety. To take its place successfully in our reflective frame, that is, to provide a rich enough logical ground for the range of phenomena that it is to account for in direct experience, water qua notion has to open up by means of an internal differentiation of its own. And heat seems to become cognitively accessible more through this internal variation made available by its relation to water than through the self-identity that we take it to have when considering it in mere logical juxtaposition with water. In other words, thinking of heat as not-water, but significantly related to water holds out some hope of coming to an understanding of the intrinsic nature of heat. Whereas, thinking of heat only in relation to not-heat offers us nothing but an empty logical construct. Obviously, the importance of the logical relation is reciprocal in this sense as well. That is, water considered in relation to not-water leaves us where we began, with the positing of a first term that might or might not turn out to be useful. It is only when we start thinking of the internal variety that logically depends on heat (now considered just as some meaningful term other than *water*) that we can move away from the first position far enough to assess the efficacy of having posited it. And this is the central logical issue.

I may seem to have belabored this primitive little schema beyond any possible use, but I am convinced that it is only in slogging through the development of such frameworks that their fundamental logical structure begins to display itself. It becomes clear as we think through the development of a relatively simple framework that no first position taken by itself will issue in anything more than a useless and cognitively opaque indeterminacy. We sometimes diguise this fact by attributing a determinacy to that first position that it cannot really support, but find as soon as we seek even a minimal account of the ground of this putative determinacy that something more is needed. Determinacy cannot stand by itself as a first position, since it requires some kind of content to make sense; and as soon as any such content is supplied, we already have two distinct terms: the content and its character (qua determination), the one just as necessary as the other. But neither can the content stand by itself, and if we try to hold that it can self-reflexively provide the ground for its own determination, the development of our account comes to an abrupt halt. In the absence of some other determination, we would have to content ourselves with a meaningless repetition of the first term in response to any question. What is? Water. How did it come to be? Water. Is there anything else? Water. What distinguishes this term as something cognitively accessible? Water. What does it do? Water. (Note that even the relatively recent suggestion about terms at this level is not really logically possible. We cannot even legitimately say "water waters" because that introduces various distinctions—active-passive, temporal—for which no groundwork has been laid.)

If no single determination will do as a ground for a fully fledged logical schema, the obvious next step would seem to be the addition of a second determination. (Or some greater plurality of determinate terms. It doesn't really matter how many, since once a ground-level plurality is introduced in any magnitude, the system will have the same logical character regardless of the number of terms posited at the outset.) But as soon as that term is proposed it enters into a logical play with the first term that gives rise to considerably more complexity than one might have anticipated. When opposition, that is, the opposition in terms of which we are at first inclined to interpret the relationship, is considered carefully, it turns out that its own nature is by no means as determinate as we intially suppose it to be. This is true in part because the opposition of the two elemental notions we have posited is responsible for drawing them together as much as for holding them apart. They are drawn together logically by the very determinacy that seems to issue from their opposition. For as determinations—or the sort of ontological structures that, from a further reflective remove, we will refer to as determinate beings—they are similar to one another, though it remains the case that their particular determinate contents are taken to be distinct. Or, to put the same point in slightly different language, as limited terms, they are least logically similar in that their character from an external point of view (i.e., from a point of view whose abstraction can neglect the individual content of the terms) is the same. And, from an equally abstract point of view, because they are limited by one another, they are drawn together still more closely (if paradoxically) by the fact of their mutual resistance. In limiting the other, each enters into the logical constitution of the other qua determination. But, as we shall see, this happens only insofar as the one that is acting as limit sloughs off its own determinate limitations and takes on an indeterminate character that is seated in *otherness*.

Consider the terms that we have been using in this preliminary investigation. While it is completely inadequate to characterize the individual concrete content of *fire* as *not-water*, it is precisely as *not-water* that fire first became useful as a logical constituent of the framework that we were attempting to develop. Water is bounded and hence defined by the *otherness* of fire. It is not the specific content of *fire* that makes it possible to identify water as a distinct term—though, from a phenomenal point of view, it may be this that first brought fire to mind as a second term—but fire considered simply as *other* that provides the needed limitation. Having recognized this, it becomes tempting to suppose that the merely other, or something like otherness per se, actually performs this limiting function, or perhaps that we should imagine ourselves to be moving toward some more sophisticated logical perspective from which it will seem reasonable to suggest that some such abstraction undergirds this more primitively defined logical frame. But otherness per se, if it means anything at all, will do us no more good as a limit than nothingness per se would. As I hinted in the earlier sections of this chapter, we may have to reconcile ourselves to the slightly discomfiting suggestion that boundaries are never themselves entirely determinate. Even so, the notion of a boundary, to be intelligible, surely requires that the terms its sets off from one another are both in some sense determinate. And as a result, the attempt to use some barren notion of otherness, that is, otherness per se, or otherness in itself, generates only a self-defeating roadblock for the possibility of developing a logical framework beyond the positing of a first term.

If we try to enrich our understanding of the first term by holding that it is determinate, and then seek some ground for that determination in the merely other, we will find ourselves forced into a decision between two equally futile logical paths. The first of these amounts to allowing the first term to explode outward in search of some limiting concept that will ultimately restrain it sufficiently to bring it back into relation with the concrete character of the direct experience it is intended to explain. But a bare notion of otherness can provide no such restraint, and we will find our original position unacceptably divorced from the concrete phenomenal ground that it is meant to recover and explain—or at least describe. The second amounts to thinking of the first term as developing in the opposite direction, that is, as turning back in on itself to discover some inherent determination that can be presented to the *other*. But if we attribute this sort of inherent or immanent determination to the first term, we at the same time exclude the possibility of any other term. Even internal differentiation is denied the first term, since it will have to become identical with determinacy, rendering the *other* meaningless, since determinacy itself is bound to what now amounts not only to the first term, but to the only possible term. (This is of course the fix that Parmenides got himself into, as we shall see presently.) There cannot be any other if reciprocity is extracted from the meaning of determinacy. In fact, it is not at all clear that there can be any *determinacy* even in some abstractly logical sense.

The notion of determination per se falls dangerously near to the same abyss of meaninglessness that opens when we try to make sense out of otherness per se. Although I believe it is possible to speak intelligibly of determinacy as a concept distinct from the determinations to which it is attributed, it seems most reasonable to suppose that when we do so, we are engaged in a peculiar logical activity something like what Peirce called "prescission." That is, we are separating—for reflective inspection—a logical element from a larger framework to which it nonetheless continues to be bound. There is reason for caution here. It is all too easy to begin to treat a term so abstracted as if it had a genuinely independent character and, in the process, remove it so far from its natural logical ground as to commit what Whitehead aptly called the "fallacy of misplaced concreteness."

VI. BOUNDARIES AND DETERMINACY

The logical problem that appears in trying to speak of determinacy independently of references to particular determinations arises in a slightly different guise when we consider the character of physical boundaries. A boundary does not have the same character as the thing it bounds any more than determinacy has the same character as particular determinations. In fact, it often turns out that we can't actually identify a phenomenal boundary without creating some other boundaries, that is, without making of it a thing that is itself bounded. It seems to me that this is true largely because *boundary* is the name for a relation, not a thing. Similarly, if *determinacy* refers to anything independent of determinations at all, it is to a certain kind of relation or series of relations that become necessary as we try to move beyond the utterance of a first term. From the broadest perspective, *determinacy* seems to be fundamentally a name for the kind of thinking that is necessary to the development of discursive frameworks. Hence it is linked to such frameworks in an essential fashion, but cannot be contained by any one of them in the sense that the terms distinguished within the framework are. Let me try to develop these suggestions by returning to the phenomenal boundaries of the earlier sections of the chapter, now considered as practical analogues for the theoretical function of determinacy in logical frameworks.

When, say, the island that I have been calling to mind is divided into separate plots of land by the stone walls, it takes on a certain character whose roots are to be found in the means and ends of practical experience. These little fields are marked out from one another by boundaries that presumably emerged quite naturally as the people who built the walls considered how much land was required to produce enough food to support a family of a particular size, how much more would provide a needed surplus as a guard against future contingencies, how much labor was available to work the land, and so on. As needs and social divisions within the family and without grew increasingly more complex, the pattern of the walls took on a more and more highly defined character. And finally, one finds in the pattern, considered now from a perspective that has distanced itself from the practical issues that formed it, an abstract image of those practical exigencies that gave rise to it. This abstract image enters into our thinking as a map that can give us reflective access to the original collection of practical exigencies in such a way as to make systematic reflection about them possible. And as we proceed with this sort of reflection, there is a great temptation to begin to imagine that the systematic character of our reflection mirrors some similar character in the ground of practical experience. When we consider the map, it certainly seems to display a system, a structured organization of bounded elements. Isn't it reasonable then to suppose that the same sort of boundedness should be attributed to the practical experience of which it is a map? And, of course, as we use the map for reflective access to that experience, it begins to seem not only reasonable but necessary to accept this supposition. The experience we are considering does indeed have a bounded character, not only in the sense that it can be distinguished from other kinds of experience—which presumably would give rise to different if analogous maps—but also in the sense that it is internally divided into bits and pieces that correspond with the means and ends identified from the initial position. Now the question is whether those divisions themselves fit into the pattern of our map. Just how close is the image to the original?

Imagine an ordinary map whose outlines trace the complex pattern of the stone walls that checker the island. It is the outlines that we are immediately concerned with here, as they depict the boundaries that we have been considering. The role that they play in the structure of the map is obviously a crucial one. Without them, there is no map. At the same time, their import has nothing of the solidity of the plots of land that they mark out in the picture. It is the plots that give the lines meaning rather than the other way round. Still, one wants to say, without the lines the plots would have no definition, and it is just the definition of the plots that makes the map a map. If asked why the map was drawn in the first place, surely the answer would be, "to mark out these bits of land." That is what the map is *for*; in short, that is what gives the map meaning. If meaning depends upon the boundaries, what sense can it make to say that they haven't the solidity of the plots of land? *Solidity* in this context amounts to meaning, doesn't it? What gives the map interest, what makes it a picture of something worth bothering about, is the meaning that we attach to those bits of land relative to the practical experience with which we began. And if it was reasonable to suppose that the little fields were established as distinct entities by boundaries that grew naturally out of that experience, then surely the boundaries have as much solidity as the experience has.

Yet on the map, the boundaries are only lines. And the map is really about spaces, not lines. In some fundamental sense, it seems to be the spaces that give the map its importance. Part of what I mean by this is again connected to the sort of questions that one imagines being asked about the map. Where is *this*? Who owns *that*? How long would it take to walk from *here* to *there*? These questions are about the spaces that are marked out, not about the lines that distinguish them. The questions that might be asked about the lines themselves are all questions that have practical significance only in relation to the spaces. What scale is being used? How accurate is the portrayal of the boundaries? The lines make the spaces visible, but the spaces give the lines their significance. The lines represent boundaries *of something*, whereas the spaces seems to have a character in themselves. Questions can be asked and answered about the spaces without direct reference to the lines, while the reverse is not true. Nevertheless, the claim that the lines make the spaces *visible* is scarcely one to be put aside as insignificant. However much we might like to say something like "the spaces would be there whether we took the trouble to draw the lines or not," (and to think that this is as much true of the original as it is of the image), it turns out that the *meaning* of the spaces as they appear on the map is intrinsically linked to the boundaries represented by the lines. *Something* might well be there without the lines, but these spaces, as representing fields that have a certain character developed and cultivated by people living a certain kind of life, would not be.

What can we learn from this? If we can learn something about boundaries by thinking about the interplay between the lines and the spaces, we may at the same time draw nearer to understanding the corresponding place of determinacy in the play between the elements of the primitive scheme we've been building with Milesian elements. But a further reflective remove is required. Three distinct elements have emerged in our thinking about the fields and the walls. There is first the experience itself, the practical concerns that stand as an originative ground; second, the map that represents the developed character of that experience by providing an abstract image of it; and, third, our reflection upon the relation between the first two. The map can function as a kind of bridge between the initial ground of experience and our attempts to come to a clear reflective appraisal of it. Now the whole point of the exercise revolves around the desire for a better understanding of the place of the boundaries that figure in each of these three reflectively distinct positions. The stone walls, the outlines of the map, the reflective distinctions, all have fundamental and crucial roles to play, but all seem on closer inspection to take on an elusive logical character that is related to the character of the *not-* in the logical interplay between water and fire as elements of the Milesian logical framework. The bound-aries, we would like to say, are *there* certainly, but not quite in the way the things (either practical or logical) that are "inside" or "outside" relative to them (or that are defined by them) are *there*.

But perhaps this "elusive character" appears only in the midst of abstract reflection. After all, what is elusive about stone walls? There they are, marching across the island, solid and timeless. Suppose we say that it is the walls qua boundaries that we are talking about, and when considered in this fashion, they seem to be independent of—in the sense of not being reducible to—any of the phenomenal descriptions that might ordinarily spring to mind. The hard-headed sentry of common sense smiles condescendingly: "I thought you were asking about the *walls*, not about some abstruse philosophical abstraction." But I want to say, it *is* the walls themselves that we are thinking of when we talk about boundaries; in fact, any set of phenomenal descriptions, however simple ("narrow piles of rocks") or complex ("fragments of carboniferous limestone whose chemical composition is . . . ") would have a much more abstract character. That is, no such description would be an appropriate response to the question "What are those things?" A meaning may seem a more abstract sort of thing than a rock, but in this case it is the meaning that gives the rock its practical solidity, not the reverse. But the meaning itself is the problem. We might force our champion of common sense to agree that what he means by "brass tacks" or the "real facts" actually has more the character of a meaning than of a lump of carbon, but we are not really much further along. When the meaning of the thing we are trying to identify turns out to be "boundary," or to stick with the more concrete and direct language that we should use here, when what a thing *is* turns out to be a boundary, a certain indeterminacy appears where we might be least inclined to expect it. Surely, one thinks, a boundary must be determinate if anything is. And just the reverse seems to be the case. Meaning seems so obviously and intimately tied to determinacy, and the notion of determinacy to that of the bounded, that when we encounter something in experience that can be best and most directly described as a boundary, it seems reasonable to expect it to give itself over at once to a clear and precise discursive analysis.

But instead, we have actually stumbled on one of those moments in reflective experience that hold out in equal parts the most interest and the most danger. We are at the beginning of systematic thought, however straightforward the questions that led us here might have seemed. We might even argue that any question whatever would ultimately bring us back to the same place, inasmuch as Wittgenstein's point that answers must come to an end somewhere—and not in some ultimate answer—is really just a recognition of the problem we are investigating. For what we mean by "meaning" is in almost all cases, practical and theoretical alike, not just tied to determinacy and boundedness, it is *identical* with these concepts. When we ask about what something means, or, for that matter, when we ask what something *is*, aren't we really asking for limits, for an unambiguous statement of the boundaries that mark off the thing in question from other things? It should not surprise us then to find that we run into tricky waters when the thing that we are asking about is that which we ordinarily take to make answers of any sort possible.

In a sense, identifying something as a boundary seems rather to extract than to contribute meaning to it; it means, among other things, that its meaning must be lodged elsewhere, in that which it bounds. If we return to the walls, seeking some more determinate understanding of what they are qua boundaries, that is, asking for a definition of what the boundaries are "in themselves," we find nothing of the determinacy that the walls quite clearly give to the fields they surround. Whether we look with a microscope or with what people once called "the mind's eye," no boundary-in-itself will appear. Neither a chemical analysis of the rocks nor the most carefully drawn outline on a map will provide us with a secure definition for "boundary" that is independent of that which is bounded. And the same thing happens in the theoretical frameworks, however simple or complex, that constitute the tradition we rely on. Those frameworks are elaborated and reconsidered from a perspective that takes their apparent determinacy for granted. And having moved away from the first moment of reflection toward the full articulation of the elaborated scheme, we seldom bother to return to reflect on the logical instruments that make that articulation possible. In fact, just to the extent that the development of these schemes requires determinacy as a foundational notion, it is itself ordinarily exempted from the kind of inspection for which it is our primary and essential tool.

VII. THE UNBOUNDED

When I talk to students about the Presocratics, speculating about the thinking that lay behind their assertions, Anaximander's *apeiron* always presents itself as a particularly interesting puzzle. It seems such an un-Milesian sort of notion. Where can it find a place in the practical and concrete thinking of these early empiricists? The unbounded, unlimited, undefined. I have often wondered whether it wasn't reflection similar to that of the last section that might finally have led Anaximander, (and not very happily), to the conclusion that some such term must be given a fundamental place in his scheme.

We might imagine him at first trying to resolve Thales' problems and hitting on the possibility of a plurality of primary elements. Nor would such a resolution have been by any means as obvious and attractive as it might seem in retrospect. Anaximander must have thought that he was treading on treacherous ground when he made such a suggestion. Unless we consider these thinkers to have been primitives as opposed to pioneers, one has to assume that they were deeply concerned about the logical character of the systems they were developing. It seems reasonable to suppose that Thales was after an *explanation*, not just a picture. And explanations require principles of development. That drive toward a unified account that will be self-consciously articulated and undertaken as Greek thought matures must have been at least implicitly operative in its earliest stages. And if one begins with a plurality, there is the clear danger that his fully articulated scheme will never discover a unifying principle that can form a One out of the initial Many. At the same time, although it might be possible to reduce the enormous variety of phenomena in ordinary experience to some small group of fundamental elements, reducing them to one, even to one as potentially rich as "water," presents insurmountable problems. It does, in any case, if one is not prepared to allow his account to deviate from direct experience so far as to make the radical distinction between reality and appearance that is to come with the Eleatics. No, one thinks of the Milesians as hard-headed empiricists, interested in a scientific account to be sure, that is, determined to move beyond a merely descriptive display of phenomena in their immediate guises, but not too far beyond. Hence the focus on natural elements as the most satisfactory first terms. And if no single term will do, the next best thing is to find some limited set that will serve as a ground.

If we can go this far in attributing reflective sophistication to them, why not also assume that a thinker like Anaximander was aware not only of the phenomenally based paradoxes that would appear if he tried to solve Thales' problems without reforming his beginning, but likewise of the logical problems? That is, if we take water as our primary term in the development of an empirical account, there is the obvious difficulty presented by fire as a sort of phenomenal antipode. Water can stand the test of difference, can subsume a great deal of the phenomenal variety that a complete account must manage to reduce, but making a place for genuine opposition is something else again. And as I was at some pains to show earlier, to say that fire stands opposed to water is to oversimplify what reflection exposes to be a rather elaborate relation, since fire is seen to enter into an interplay with its "opposite" that affects even the internal structure of the other. But in thinking about that complex interplay, the logical reading of the problem also appears. The ultimate unity that we hope to find in the development of an account must have not only a reasonable phenomenal ground—of the sort provided, for example, by the fact that water appears naturally in all three physical forms—but must also have a sufficiently rich *logical* foundation. There must be something in the logical constitution of the first term that can support the differences within unity that we hope to introduce as the reflective analogue of the phenomenal variety of direct experience. And to provide a foundation for this differentiation, the first term must itself have a determinate character. Being determinate seems to require boundaries or limits, and that means that we have to find something to provide such boundaries. There has to be some other term, since we have discovered that determinacy-in-itself is unable to stand on its own as a concept with a meaning independent of the contents of the terms that it circumscribes. Hence Anaximander proposes a plurality—but only to find that this does not, at least in itself, solve the problem.

The complexity of the relations among the terms of the plurality requires more than a simple statement of their individual characters. Such a statement, if it is to avoid Thales' problem, must incorporate the logical notions that make the distinctions among the elements possible. That is, it requires not only a distinction among the elements themselves, but also a distinction between the bounded and the unbounded. I suspect that this is just what Anaximander intended to include with the idea of the *apeiron*. What holds these elements together is not determinacy, but indeterminacy. It is after all determinacy that holds them apart where *determinacy* is understood in its most straightforward sense, as something like "boundedness" or "limitation." But what holds them together in the complex interplay that can give rise to something more than a mere plurality, that can develop into the sort of system that offers an explanation, is not itself determinate. Water, fire, earth, and air considered as discrete elements will become useful as primary terms in a system only when they are considered in relation to one another, though such a consideration certainly entails a careful analysis of their individual characters. In fact, it is just such an analysis that might have led Anaximander to posit the unbounded as an originative ground. Opposition of the sort found in the relation between water and fire or earth and air includes reciprocity in its nature, and the very relation that was taken to hold these elements apart now draws them together in the bonds of logical definition. The boundaries between them are as real as the stone walls, but, just as in the case of the walls, these boundaries (considered independently) seem to defy attempts at ordinary definition.

Water and fire are separated both phenomenally and logically, but the boundary that separates them is intelligible only in relation to the separation it is taken to denote. It is not itself something that has the definition of either of the terms that it stands between. Since we cannot argue that this means that water is reducible to fire or that the reverse is true without landing ourselves back in Thales' boat, we are stuck with assuming that something else has entered the picture. Or, to put the point more accurately, a logical concept has been uncovered in our scheme that has a character quite different from that of the primary terms themselves.

If water is to be determinate, there must be some Other that can give "not-water" a meaning. But if we try to turn fire into such an other, and suppose that we have discovered the internal structure of fire by characterizing it as "not-water," we will encounter the sort of problem discussed previously. Fire (or, for these purposes, indifferently earth or air) then, must be both something in itself *and* "not-water" to allow for the further development of the account. That is, it (or any one of the other elements when considered in relation to *its* others) must appear both as something determinately in itself and something indeterminately but meaningfully distinct from water in order to take its place in the scheme. As a term in the system, it is both determinate and indeterminate, and if the scheme is to have any logical efficacy as regards the goal of an explanatory account that incorporates difference and unity, both of these logical characters must be maintained as irreducible aspects of its logical nature.

I suppose it is obvious that I am stealing up on the Platonic understanding of otherness as it appears in similar contexts. In his later work, most directly in the *Sophist*, Plato will show that the *not-* that holds terms apart in relational frameworks of this sort has a relative character, and that it can be translated into "otherness" as a way of distinguishing it from the more severe understanding of negation that led Parmenides to argue that not-being has no place in an intelligibly discursive account. But I think—and shall argue more directly in the next chapter—that even Plato neglects some of the implications of the logical character of the sort of "otherness" that has entered into our scheme of things. In some ways it is easier to consider this character in the logically more sophisticated terms of the "major classes" (*megista gene*) that provide the context for Plato's discussion, but I think it is important to think about the place and character of otherness in this relatively simple context first.

I note again that I am thinking of the Milesian scheme of things in the light of the developments to come and as a result may be attributing to Anaximander an insight that did not figure in his thinking at all. When he proposes the *apeiron* as the fundamental term in his elemental framework, he may have been merely dodging the problems that arise when one tries to use a single determination as the ground of an account that can do equal justice to unity and plurality. Having decided that a plurality of coequally fundamental elements is required to reconcile his account with the phenomena, Anaximander may well have simply imposed the *apeiron* as a unifying deus ex machina. But if that were the case, why use this particular notion? *Apeiron*. The unbounded, the unlimited, the undefined. Why not, for example, simply insist that the four basic elements are drawn together in the One or the Whole, both of which notions were certainly available to him as alternatives? Why the *Apeiron?*

Our knowledge of the period does not provide an historical answer to this question, but it may be that we have already been providing a logical one. Whatever Anaximander's reasons or intentions, his use of the term *apeiron* points to a foundational tension in the underpinning of any logical framework. Such frameworks become useful only to the extent that they can provide us with a system of differentiation, but they must also provide some larger sense in which the differences marked out within them are drawn back together, if not into some all-encompassing unity, then at least into significant and internal relation with one another. A framework of sheerly discrete elements is not really a framework at all; it is merely a collection. It is in the interplay among the elements of a logical scheme that the scheme provides a useful abstract image of the relations among the phenomena that we set out to describe, and that interplay demands determinacy as the undergirding for intelligible differentiation. But there seems to be no way of introducing this determinacy into the framework without at the same time giving rise to a certain indeterminacy. In order to bound one element, we need some Other, but this Other must itself have some meaningful content if it is to function as the logical ground of the boundary between whatever two elements we are considering. As soon as we give the second element this content, however, we distinguish it as something that also requires an Other as a bounding notion and the same will hold true for any number of elements.

Now our inclination, as the result of long logical practice, is to assume that the determinacy on which all of this rests, the determinacy that makes it possible even to consider such a system from an abstract perspective, is something carried into the system by the particular content of the elements. But if that were true, there would be no ground for the reciprocal nature of the relations among the elements, and it is in that reciprocity that the concept of a boundary first becomes cognitively accessible. As we have seen, boundaries considered in themselves, the notion of a boundary qua boundary leads to tail-chasing just as useless as thinking about "determinacy-in-itself" or "otherness per se." Boundaries lie between things, but are not *things* themselves, at least if we use the term *thing* in its ordinary sense, since it is typically taken to connote a determinacy that is itself defined in terms of boundaries. Neither can some particular determinate content (some *determination* as the term was used previously) provide the ground for determinacy in general since in doing so, that content would disappear into the trackless waste of sheer relativity. How then can we provide a foundation for determinacy? What logical structure can provide it with the definition that it will in turn provide to the expanding set of determinations by means of which our systems will take on theoretical import and practical efficacy? What can bound the bounded? *The Apeiron.* The unbounded, the unlimited, the undefined.

CHAPTER 3

BEING, NOT-BEING, AND THE OTHERNESS OF OTHERNESS

The end of our foundation is the knowledge of causes, and secret motions of things; and the enlarging of the bounds of human Empire, to the effecting of all things possible.

Francis Bacon, *New Atlantis*

I. THE REFLECTIVE REMOVE

So far we have been thinking about determinacy and related issues in terms of direct experience and the simplest kind of reflective frameworks that might develop out of it. Now it is time to take a very cautious step back from direct experience and to adopt a perspective sufficiently abstract to allow a clear view of the ontological structure of the relation between determinacy and indeterminacy. The point of view that has traditionally been called "metaphysical," sometimes in admiration, sometimes with disdain, has to be taken up if the kind of question that we have been asking is to have any answer. I make a point of saying this because it is just at the juncture we have reached that we are too often inclined to pull back from a full investigation of fundamental ontological issues, turning our attention instead to the intricacies of empirical analysis. While I certainly do not mean to suggest that empirical analysis is inappropriate or unprofitable, it does seem to me that we have sometimes found ourselves puzzled by the results of this kind of analysis not so much because of any inherent paradox presented by the phenomena themselves as because of our own inadequate understanding of the logical presuppositions that shape both the analysis and, more importantly, our interpretation of its results. We are puzzled less by the phenomena than by the way that they seem to continue to wriggle out of the categorial nets that we weave to contain them.

Our most common response has been to assume that some tighter weave will make a difference, that some more careful method of observation and the corollary production of more highly refined categories will solve the problem. And in one sense, this has proved extremely fruitful—we know a great deal more about the world than the Milesians did. But in another sense, we seem to have made little progress indeed. The ancient standoff between the One and the Many, the play between sameness and difference as we try to reconcile our experience of plurality with our desire for unity, leads to as many logical puzzles and theoretical battles now as it did then. Or, to refer to what amounts to the same tension characterized in rather loftier terms, we are as puzzled about the relation between Being and Becoming, the Eternal and the Temporal as the ancients were, though outside the world of professional philosophy, such questions are normally taken up in quite different language.[1]

The fact that these basic ontological tensions and conflicts remain despite enormous advances on other fronts leads me to believe that there must be something that lies neglected at the most fundamental level of our practice in thought. And if any new light is to be shed on the structure of our thought at this level, the reflective remove that makes metaphysical discourse possible is required, however uneasy we may have become with what we once took for granted as "first philosophy." The trick is to find a way of stepping back without losing touch with the concrete character of the earlier moments of our investigation. Nor is this actually so difficult a thing to do. In the light of the historical developments of the tradition, we have grown accustomed to supposing that there is a necessary disjunction between direct observation and experimentation on the one hand, and metaphysical speculation on the other. (One thinks of Wittgenstein's characterization of the philosopher as someone too lazy to work in a laboratory.) In fact, this notion has seeped so deeply into our thinking that "metaphysics" has come to refer to everything from the bizarre speculations of "parapsychology" to the delusions of people under the influence of psychedelic drugs. Still worse, it has led the defenders of "common sense," having dismissed systematic reflection as the private entertainment of a misguided few, to neglect the logical roots of their own positions.

Although I believe that it is critical never to lose sight of the direct experience in which our more abstract analyses are grounded, there comes a

---

1. I have in mind, for example, disputes concerning the viability of a unified field theory, or the apparent conflict between the irreversibility of biochemical processes and the supposedly reversible character of time as characterized in both classical and relativity physics. Or, thinking again in broad strokes, the increasingly apparent tension between the mechanistic models of early modern science and the more recent introduction in physical as well as biological science of evolutionary and organically based models. But this is the sort of issue that I shall be taking up in more detail in the third book of this study.

point in reflection when we must try to free ourselves of the concerns of immediate experience, and explore the ontological structure of the thinking that develops out of those concerns. In this chapter, I shall be adopting such a perspective, continuing to focus on the play between determinacy and indeterminacy as this crucial relation appears in the more abstract reflection that developed out of the ideas of the Milesians. Here again, I shall be using a quasi-historical approach, thinking first through the general framework of Parmenides' ideas and then taking up a consideration of the more completely articulated metaphysical scheme in Plato's later work. However, the point of this chapter is not chiefly to illuminate the work of either thinker. It is rather to try to explore the ontological roots of the relation between determinacy and indeterminacy with a view toward exposing the foundation of our bias toward the determinate dimensions of thought and being and our continuing neglect of the importance of indeterminacy in the ontological structure of both orders. As we take up a careful speculative examination of concepts like being and not-being with a view to uncovering the logic of determinacy and indeterminacy, we are not separating ourselves illegitimately from the direct experience with which we began, but considering one of its most basic characters. For what we normally mean by "direct experience" is actually a dialogue with the world that is already fraught with hidden presuppositions, some of the most deeply embedded of which surround the central but inadequately explored place of the relation between determinacy and indeterminacy in our thought and practice.

II. BEING AND BOUNDARIES

a. Being and Nothing

While the Milesians took a very important first step, it is with Parmenides that abstract speculation becomes genuinely and reflectively self-conscious. In his work we find the first direct attempt to uncover the logical foundations of speculative thought as he tries to come to terms with the hardest and most profound of human questions. What is real? Is there some truth to be located and understood in the midst of the flux of ordinary experience? If we are after a coherent conception of the whole, what logical alternatives are open to us? Parmenides' answer seems fairly straightforward: there are only two routes to be taken, "the one, that it is and that it is not possible for it not to be . . . ; the other, that it is not and that it is right for it not to be . . . " The second route, the path of Not-being, as he goes on to argue, is completely uninformative and leads rather away from than toward "Persuasion and Truth." Hence we are left with the task of examining more closely the only genuine option, the path of Being. But it turns out that this examination is by no means as straightforward a task as it might have seemed and, in fact, that even the distinction between the two routes is not really as clear as it at first appeared to be.

If we assume, as nearly everyone always has, that Parmenides intended to begin with a distinction between Being and Nothing, some very difficult logical problems immediately arise. Consider Parmenides' first argument in defense of his assertion that there is only one path to be taken: "for you could not know what is not—for that is not possible—nor say it."[2] Here and in the passages that follow, Parmenides binds logic itself not only to being, but to a particular understanding of being. And this is true whether the identity between νοεῖν and εἶναι is understood to be tentative or ultimate in this fragment. Although interesting comments concerning the development of the argument of the poem can be made based on varying interpretations of this relation, the fundamental logical point remains the same.[3] Parmenides is insisting that if you are to think, you must think about *something*, for thinking about nothing amounts to the same thing as not thinking at all.

What could be more reasonable? Of course there is no point in trying to think about nothing. Why would we try to do so in the first place? And if we are silly enough to do so, we have obviously set off on a path that by its own definition leads nowhere. The trouble is that we *do* think about nothing from time to time, at least we philosophers do, and Parmenides himself is thinking about nothing at the very moment that his goddess issues an injunction against such thinking. Nor does it seem likely that the father of Western logic was unaware of this little irony. Now given that Parmenides is quite certainly thinking about "nothing," the real question is just what is it that he is thinking about? Obviously, he can't be thinking about nothing, as we might say, simpliciter. Focusing on nothing is the same as focusing on everything, which is the same as not focusing at all. This is just the sort of nonsense that people unacquainted with philosophy suppose that philoso-

---

2.   οὔτε γὰρ ἂν γνοίης τό γε μὴ ἐόν (οὐ γαρ ἀνυστόν)οὔτε φράσαις. Fr. 2:7–8. (Here and hereafter I shall refer to the text using the arrangement of the fragments found in David Gallop, *Parmenides of Elea: Fragments, A Text and Translation*, [Toronto: University of Toronto Press], pp. 48ff., though I shall ordinarily use my own translations.) I think that it continues to be reasonable to complete this line with the fragment, τὸ γὰρ αὐτὸ νοεῖν ἐστίν τε καὶ εἶναι, fr. 3, ("for thought and being are the same"), though doing so seems to have fallen out of fashion—see, for example, Kirk and Raven, *The Presocratic Philosophers*, (Cambridge: Cambridge University Press, 1983), p. 246, f.n. 2. It is in any case clear here and in what follows, (cf. fr. 6), that Parmenides considers the relation between thought and being to be crucial to his argument.

3.   For an excellent discussion of this and related points, see Scott Austin, *Parmenides: Being, Bounds, and Logic* (New Haven, Conn.: Yale University Press, 1986), esp. Ch. 4.

phers come up with. Actually, Parmenides has already told us what he is
thinking about, since in his view, there *is* only one thing to think about.
When he thinks about "nothing," which is really to say, when he juxtaposes
this notion with Being as a way of introducing the extremely hard-headed
logic that forms the center of his argument, he must be thinking about Being. I do not in the least mean to suggest that he is arguing for something
like the identity of Being and Nothing in the Hegelian sense.[4] Rather, it
seems most reasonable to suppose that he is using the relation between Being and Nothing to set the stage for the characterization of Being that is to
come. When we have put aside the ἔθος πολύπειρον, the "long-standing
habit" of confusing what-is with what-is-not, of thinking that the same thing
both is and is not in what the goddess takes to be the ordinary way of mortals, it will become possible to understand the true nature of what-is as logic
carries us along the path not only of Persuasion, but of Truth. Following this
path, we are presented with the familiar characterization of Absolute Being.
It is what it is: timeless, immovable, indivisible, beginningless and endless,
immanently coherent, utterly complete.

Putting aside for the moment some of the enormous problems that Parmenides is prepared to dismiss rather cavalierly (notably, the "dousing" of
Becoming), I should like to focus on the place of negativity in his characterization of Being. As many have noted before, however much the goddess
is pleased to abjure any talk or thought about nothing, negation plays a central and critical role in nearly everything that she has to say about Being. In
fact, almost all of the important characterizations of Being are either put in
negative language to begin with, or followed immediately by some reference
to what is not. Now this scarcely introduces "Nothing" in the sense of a lacuna into the internal structure of Being, but it does give rise to an interesting play between the two notions in Parmenides' thought. It doesn't
seem possible to say anything much about Being without using negation as
a way of making sense out of our claims.

Unless we are willing to content ourselves with uttering a single word
over and over again, it seems necessary to talk about what Being is by considering it in relation to what it is not. And what it is not, if it were really
identical with nothing simpliciter, could serve no logical purpose. The fact
that it *does* serve such a purpose, and not merely a linguistic one, leads to a
reexamination of the claim that we cannot think about what-is-not. Not only
can we think about it, it turns out that we have to think about it in order to
think about what-is, at least if we mean by *what-is* what Parmenides seems
to mean. (That is, NOT-divided, NOT-moving, NOT-deficient, etc. Even

---

4.   It is, however, well worth noting that it is this very argument, together the
Platonic response to it that lays the groundwork for the Hegelian analysis in the *Science of Logic*.

characterizations that could be put much more simply in positive terms turn up in negative ones: οὐκ ἀτελεύτητον, NOT-imperfect; οὔτε γὰρ οὐκ ἐόν ἐστι, neither is it non-existing . . .) At this point, it is tempting to dismiss the whole business as leading into a futile circularity. But even if there were no other reason, Parmenides' place in the tradition makes it impossible to do so. No matter how many difficulties are involved in unraveling it, the logic of his poem—together with the difficulties—has continued to play a critical role in shaping the form and content of systematic speculation.

b. Being and Thought

At the center of Parmenides' poem, having traveled down the "path of Truth," we find ourselves thinking about what-is-not, however repugnant such a notion might have seemed at the beginning of the path. What is it that leads us into such a predicament? It seems to me that at least part of the answer to this question is to be found in Parmenides' understanding of the relation between being and thought—an understanding that will inform the thought of the next century and, through it, the basic presuppositions of the entire tradition. As soon as Parmenides links thinking and being, any characterization of Being that follows will obviously be affected by his understanding of the nature of thought. And thought, at least the kind of thought that Parmenides has in mind, requires definite boundaries.

Truth is distinguished from mere opinion primarily by the contingent character of the latter. Not only is opinion formed in accord with what both is and is not, its own changeable nature mirrors the character of its content. Hence, Parmenides assumes that if he is to make his distinction between truth and opinion stick, he must attribute an unchanging character to Truth. In order to do that, he has to show that what-is (or what the Truth is about) is utterly stable. Movement of any kind will be considered anathema from the perspective of Truth, and this must hold especially in regard to any movement that might be attributed to the boundaries of what-is. What better way to make this point than to bound what-is with movement itself? And this is exactly what Parmenides does. "What-is is ungenerable and unperishing, a whole of a single kind, unmoving, and perfect."[5] Just as the goddess's speech about being is bounded all around by her warnings concerning the dangerous illusions of mortal opinion, so is Being itself bounded by a series of intrinsically indeterminate concepts. Mutability, divisibility, variation of any sort, all have to be excluded if Being is to maintain its distinction from what-is-not, if Truth is to be successfully distinguished from the shadowy illusions of opinion.

---

5.   Gallop, fr. 8:3–4

Since it is directly related to the central point of this essay, I shall take up some further discussion of the place of motion in Parmenides' logical scheme in a moment. But first there is a broader issue that requires attention if we are to avoid unnecessary confusion. If we are to think along with Parmenides, we must first try to free ourselves of the various biases that any experience with the tradition naturally imposes on us. It might be rather pointless to try to call up the world of southern Italy as it was five centuries before Christ, supposing that in doing so we would gain some deeper insight into the logical structure of Parmenides' thought, but it is equally foolish to allow displeasure with later variations to deafen us to the clear and uncluttered tones of the original statement of his theme. While it is impossible to divorce oneself entirely from the history of attempts to thrash our way through the same problems, there is nothing to be gained by reducing (or enlarging) this early speech to one of those attempts and then dismissing it with one of the familiar arguments—say, Aristotle's against Plato, or Peirce's against Hegel, or, for that matter, Dr. Johnson's against whoever he thought was inclined to doubt the reality of rocks.

All of this sprang to mind as I found myself searching for a way of characterizing those things—entities? structures? concepts? forms?—that lie outside the boundaries of what-is as it is discussed in the center of Parmenides' poem. One of the things that makes Parmenides' logic so difficult to grasp is the extremely slippery relation between thought and being as the two figure in his thinking. He seems to feel none of our modern inclination to divorce one from the other, and as a result sees no reason to offer a method of reconciliation. His assertions typically carry both ontic and epistemic import, and while the emphasis shifts from one to the other, the movement is always fluid, free of the categorial barriers constructed by the modern tradition. Still, even if Parmenides is right to suppose that thought and being coincide in the sense of being two ways of considering the same thing, there must remain *some* distinction between them, and the lines along which that distinction is drawn are extremely important.

When we think from the center of the poem outward, it seems reasonable to draw a fairly clear line between thought and being since we are thinking from the perspective of a sort of hypostatized Being, the core of what-is, toward its "outermost bound,"[6] and in order to do so, there must be some sense in which what lies outside that bound is available to thought. Here being and thought must be distinct, since this thinking that looks outward toward the dark path of opinion cannot be identical with what-is. If it were, it would be impossible even to consider such a path, let alone choose to stumble along it; and besides, if such a choice is not possible, what sense can

6. πεῖρας πύματον, Gallop fr. 8:42

be made of the goddess's injunction? At the same time, being and thought are drawn together into immediate relation both at the beginning of the poem, (as quoted previously) and at its very center. Consider the line quoted in footnote 2: τὸ γὰρ αὐτὸ νοεῖν ἐστίν τε καὶ εἶναι. Heidegger may not be far wrong when he claims that this "saying becomes the basic theme for all Western-European thinking."[7] There are various ways of translating this line, each offering a slightly different slant on Parmenides' intention. Until recently, this line has typically been translated quite directly to read: " . . . for thought and being are the same."[8] While it is certain that Parmenides intends to establish a necessary link between logical thought and what-is, such a link does not by any means imply the simple identity of thought and being.[9] In fact, Parmenides could not have considered thought and being identical in the simple and straightforward sense. If they were, the poem could not have been written at all, let alone as an argument against another possible way of trying to think. Still, Parmenides clearly does intend to bind the kind of thinking that the goddess is recommending to Being, and to distinguish it from wrong thinking as thinking about what-is as opposed to thinking about what-is-not. He doesn't really say that the other path is impossible in this section of the poem, just that we will not learn anything by following it. If we want to know, we must focus on what-is.

Suppose now we translate the line in a slightly different way: "for to think what-is and to be what-is are the same." Here, I am taking ἐστίν as having the same meaning that it has in the goddess's original statement of alternatives. The problem, of course, is to come to terms with the relation between ἐστίν and εἶναι as they appear in the line. A raft of anachronistic

---

7.   Martin Heidegger, *What Is Called Thinking,* (New York: Harper and Row, 1968), p. 242.

8.   More recent translators (Gallop, Shofield) have preferred a less direct connection between the two and read the line as meaning "for the same thing is there for thinking and for being," or "for the same thing is there both to be thought of and to be." I take it that recent translating wisdom must have it that ἐστίν means "it is there" and carries existential import, instead of just functioning as a copula. It certainly sometimes seems to mean this, but I see no reason to suppose that it always does, but neither have I any interest in entering into a linguistic dispute on the matter.

9.   The more recent translation, for example, could be taken to mean something like "thinking and being share a single domain," or perhaps, "thinking and being are directed toward the same thing"—what thing, one wonders though, if it is neither thought nor being. While I take it that this newer translation is intended to clear the muddied waters of the older one, frankly I have trouble making much sense out of it. Actually, I suspect that it is founded in a not very carefully examined modern fear of any breach in the wall between thought and being.

possibilities occur to mind. It wouldn't be entirely unreasonable to take εἶναι to mean something like essence in the Aristotelian sense and then to interpret Parmenides' assertion as meaning that the essence of what-is is identical with the thought of what-is. The essence of being [the real] is identical with genuine thought [the truth]. He certainly means something like this, but not, for example, what an absolute idealist would mean in making the same assertion. Perhaps it is best for the moment to take up the simplest interpretation as the most accurate. If you intend to think true thoughts, then you must think about what-is, not about what-is-not. Such a recommendation was, one assumes, as much tied to direct experience then as it would be now if one were speaking, say, to a child—or in any case not philosophizing. The truth is bound to what-is, the false to what-is-not; when we say that something is true, we mean that it is the case, something that is false is not the case.

Now the poem is at least as much about Thought as it is about Being; in fact, if either is a secondary notion, I would argue that it is the latter. After all, the whole point of the journey taken by the narrator is to try to discover the truth. But it turns out that in order to do so, we have to start off by making a curious distinction between what-is and what-is-not. It is essential to bear in mind how that distinction initially came into focus as we go on to consider the complex characterizations of what-is, or of Being, that will develop in the consideration of the goddess's alternatives. Parmenides is simply trying to point the way toward a kind of thinking that will avoid some of the pitfalls of "mortal opinion" and starts with some fundamental distinctions that he thought would smooth the path toward that end. Reasonably enough, he associates change with confusion and goes on to characterize Being (what-is true) with that which is exempt from change or variation of any sort. That about which we can think clearly "remains the same and in the same place," staying "steadfast on the spot."[10]

When thought and being are linked here in the center of the poem, it is to make a point about genuine thought, not really about being at all. As we consider Parmenides' point here, it is crucial to remember that at the most fundamental level of reflection there cannot be any very clear distinction between being and thought, simply because it is a level logically prior to that at which such distinctions become useful. We are so accustomed to assuming that such a distinction can be taken as itself a ground-level position that it may at first seem rather bizarre to suggest that it is not. Or, it may seem that to suggest that the distinction between thought and being is itself a function of thought already leans too much toward idealism. If the distinction between thought and being is itself a thought, being collapses into thought and

---

10.   Gallop, fr. 8:29–30

the Absolute Idea looms large. But this is certainly not what I mean, and I don't think that it is what Parmenides meant either.

Thought and Being are linked again in a rather difficult line, similar to the earlier one, that casts a slightly different light on their relation: ταὐτὸν δ'ἐστὶ νοεῖν τε καὶ οὕνεκεν ἐστι νόημα.[11] Though there are problems in translating it, I take this line to mean: "to think what-is [i.e., to follow the path recommended by the goddess at the outset] is the same as that about which there is [i.e., can be] thought." Thinking what-is, as we already know, amounts to following the path of Persuasion and Truth, as distinct from falling into the traps that lie on the alternative path. It is, in short, genuine thinking, logical thinking, right thinking. As such, Parmenides is obviously already assuming that it is different from, and superior to, whatever other kind of thinking we might (however foolishly) try to engage in. And if such a judgment can be made at all, it has to be made in accord with some criterion.

The normal criterion for distinctions of this sort in ordinary experience is the content (for want of a better word) of the thought in question, and it seems to me that the same criterion is being used here. The content of genuine thought is what-is. That is what makes it genuine, true, right. And it is just in this sense that the kind of thinking that Parmenides is recommending to us is the same as what it is about. He does not have to hold that thought itself is identical with what-is. In fact, far from it, the whole point of the argument is to distinguish one kind of thinking from another, and if that distinction is to be made, it has to be possible at least to conceive of thought independently of what-is. The path that the goddess recommends to us may be the only true one, but it cannot be the only possible one. Not only is there another possible path, in fact, but she has a good deal to say about it—albeit with various caveats attached. This reading also seems to mesh with the next line where Parmenides amplifies the point by saying οὐ γὰρ ἄνευ τοῦ ἐόντος, ἐν ὧι πεφατισμένον ἐστίν, εὑρήσεις τὸ νοεῖν. This is very straightforward: "for without being, in which it has been expressed, you will not find thought." Here again, we have to assume that he means not just thought, but *genuine* thought. Thinking is the expression of being; genuine thought is thought about what is. The truth is expressed in Being, and

---

11.   Gallop, fr. 8:34. In their first edition, Kirk and Raven had this as "what can be thought is only the thought that it is," whereas Austin translates it as meaning "the same thing is for thinking and is also that for the sake of which there is thought" (Austin, p. 165). As Austin points out, disputes about this line generally center on the meaning of οὕνεκεν. It is this that he translates as "for the sake of which," and it ends in giving his translation a curious sound in English. Much as with the earlier line, I am sympathetic to the reasons for rejecting the overly simple translation, but I have trouble making sense out of his alternative.

that is what genuine thought has to be about. Hence to understand and distinguish genuine thought from mortal opinion, Parmenides must further define Being.

c. *Being and Movement*

In the proem, Parmenides' initial focus is turned toward different ways of thinking about the world, albeit from an unworldly perspective, and it is in distinguishing those ways of thinking one from another that the discussion concerning the nature of being becomes important. The various characterizations of being that one finds at the center of the goddess's "trustworthy" speech, are not just incidentally, but *equally* characterizations of thought. And of course, they are characterizations of genuine thought, not just of thought in the broad sense of the word. A new distinction opens up here, and it is one that will reverberate throughout the entire tradition that is to follow. Genuine thinking is distinguished from the muddle of mortal opinion in terms of its content: the first concerns itself with what-is, the second with what-is-not, or with a combination of what-is and what-is-not—which amounts to the same thing. What follows after the statement of the two paths, then, can be taken as an expansion of the original characterization of the route that the goddess recommends. The route of inquiry that "it is and that it is not possible for it not to be" is the route that will lead us to "the unmoving temper of persuasive Truth." So that when the account of the route (μῦθος ὁδοῖο) unfolds, we are hearing an account not only of the nature of Being, but of the nature of Truth. The earlier link between thought and being is now refined and elucidated in a careful analysis of what-is, of the content of genuine, or what we might as well call henceforth, logical thought. We are offered a description of what logical thought is about, which, at this fundamental level of inquiry, is the same thing as an account of what logical thought *is*.

I suggested earlier that, for Parmenides, it is movement itself that bounds Being, and it is time now to return to that issue. I hope that it is clear from the outset that I intend to use *movement* in the broadest possible sense, to include variation of any sort, though our primary focus at the moment will be variation in thought. The goddess introduces her μῦθος of what-is by asserting starkly that it is ungenerated and unperishing, a whole of a single kind,[12] unmoving, and perfect.[13] What-is is cut off from change of any sort, held by necessity within immutable bounds.

---

12.   οὖλον μουνογενές, which I understand, especially in view of later comments concerning its cohesive nature, to mean "internally undifferentiated," though logically distinct comments can be made about it from an external point of view.

13.   The end of the line is disputed, but there appears to be good reason to think that one of the possible variants for 'perfect,' τελέστον, τελεῖον, τελήεν, must

While it seems to me that every line of this part of the poem is well worth careful analysis, so rich and fertile is the language, I mean to focus primarily on the character of the boundaries that Parmenides seems to have in mind. We have been looking at boundaries in a wide variety of contexts so far, but this one is particularly important to the larger thrust of this study, because it is here that we find the first self-conscious attempt to establish the boundaries of discursive thought itself. When Parmenides' goddess marks out the limits of the route of inquiry that we are to follow, she delimits not only the kind of question that can be asked, but also the kind of answer that will be considered acceptable. We are to associate with the Truth, with the proper path of reflection, only that which is utterly stable and perfectly bounded. While it is difficult (if not impossible) to think or to speak without wandering outside these bounds, we are told that when we do so, we are departing from the truth, and following a path that leads at most to a semblance of order.

This brings us to the crucial question. Is logical thought possible without a consideration of whatever it is that lies on the other side of the boundaries of Being? For all of his stern warnings, Parmenides both introduces and closes his "trustworthy" account with direct references to its purportedly "untrustworthy" alternative. Moreover, as we have already seen in passing, much of the language that he uses to characterize Being is lodged in the terms of the dark path of negativity. Why? To answer in the most direct terms: because he must. There is no way to point to, let alone define and reflectively examine, the utterly stable without thinking about it in relation to what is not stable. And this logical correlate, if it is to serve its purpose, must be taken to have some sort of positive content. In order to meaningfully characterize something as changeless, change must have at least a conceptually positive character. Trying to define change in merely negative terms, as something like a lack of changelessness, will not lead anywhere. For one thing, that expression is entirely empty of content; double negation becomes a useful concept only when conjoined with position, and the position here is what is in question. But still more importantly, the sheer fact of change in ordinary experience (in its reflective and unreflective dimensions alike) militates against such a logical reduction.

In the midst of abstract reflection, while we are trying to balance one concept against another, imposing order on what sometimes seems a recalcitrantly disorderly array of ideas, it is easy to forget the steps that led us to such a position in the first place. In order to make reflection of this

---

have completed it. In any case, the line certainly prefigures the emphasis upon completeness and boundedness at the end of the account of what-is in lines 8:42–49. See Gallop for alternate readings.

sort possible, we must already have moved from one position to another. It may well be that reflective activity is a natural and fundamental element in the human response to the world, but it is identified at least in the beginning as a separation from the immediate concerns of brute existence, a movement away from the world that it will assess. And ordinarily, even in reflection of the most rudimentary kind, it is a movement away from change in search of changelessness. Lost in the immediate world of apparently limitless variation, we seek something stable, some unchanging ground from which we can get our bearings. And we find it, of course. Certain regularities, similarities, recurrences begin to emerge and to impress themselves upon our awareness. The contours of the appearances continue to shift, but as we gain control of our focus, we find that where one sameness called itself to our attention, lending form and thereby meaning to a part of the field, others always appear, developing into a larger and increasingly useful pattern of relationships. The dance of the appearances continues, but no longer as a blur of confused and shapeless images. What might have seemed random movement takes on direction and form as each newly exposed figure of the dance calls our attention to still others, the whole seeming to be more and more a thing orchestrated by design. But these figures and forms, directions and meanings, are not there for immediate awareness. They are all creatures of reflective mediation, becoming evident only at a remove.

Even when those patterns have become hypostatized and articulated as the laws and principles of complex reflective schemata, there is movement. Reflection is, after all, an activity; and the consideration of the products of the first remove requires a further remove, a new positioning that is taken up only to be superseded by some other. And within each of these positions, there is more movement as the principles out of which they are formed are reviewed through composition and division, reshaped in the light of alternative perspectives into forms both familiar and surprisingly new. Anyone who has engaged in the game at all knows that it has a vitality all its own, that the most serene reflective discourse is often the product of an intense and furious struggle. A logical position that attempted to deny movement a meaningful place would be a precarious position indeed. And yet, at the very beginning of Western logic—perhaps not least because it *is* the beginning—we find Parmenides apparently prepared to do just that. In a few lines, he dismisses change, movement, variation of any sort as having to do only with what-is-not, as elements of a path that leads to illusion and deception. Now unless we are ready to suppose that one of the founders of logical discourse had entirely lost touch with an essential feature of his own invention, I think we have to assume that this "dismissal" is intended as a qualified one. But whatever his intentions, movement permeates both the form and content of his poem.

Far from disappearing into the murky depths of what-is-not, movement appears in crucial passages throughout the poem as a limiting notion. Parmenides begins with movement, as the immortal charioteers draw the narrator away from the world of mortal opinion toward the realm of the truth, in what is presumably an image of the repositioning required for abstract reflection of any kind. We separate ourselves from immediate concerns, as we would typically say, by taking a step back and adopting a different perspective. But that stepping back, while it is intended to separate us from movement, is itself simply a movement of a different sort. And once having adopted this new position, we find ourselves confronted with activity once again. Developing a logical account of experience requires the active work of the intellect; it is not accomplished by merely laying oneself open to the music of the spheres.

Most importantly, once having begun to develop some account of what-is, we have to return to a consideration of the steps that led us to that account, since they are also a part of the world that we are trying to describe. This is why the goddess insists that we must learn *everything;* that is, "both the unmoving temper of the truth and the opinions of mortals." If we are to come to terms with the truth, we must also come to terms with the path that leads us to it. The point that I want to emphasize now begins to take on some shape. It is not only that we must take account of opinion because it is a part of what-is in the direct sense. It is also necessary because "what-is" becomes logically available only in contradistinction from opinion, which is, for Parmenides, composed equally of what-is and what-is-not. The temper of the Truth may be unmoving, but its stability becomes conceptually accessible only through motion, through the activity of reflective discourse, and becomes logically articulable only when considered as distinct from that which is not stable. What we sometimes ignore in this familiar play of contrary notions is that the relation is not an even one when we are speaking of these particular notions. If we characterize what-is in the way that Parmenides does, as that which is utterly immutable, indivisible, undifferentiated, in short, as entirely determinate, the contrary notion that is required to make sense out of our characterization must be indeterminate. And it is by no means a notion that is identical with not-being in the sense of being empty of content. In fact, it is a term equally rich in meaning, since its meaning is derived from the contraries that Parmenides has already been using in his description of what-is. It is movement, division and composition, generation and destruction, irregularity, inconsistency: it is, in short, the unbounded. In order to make being determinate, Parmenides requires boundaries, and the boundaries themselves cannot be determinate without collapsing into being and drawing the possibility of making sense of our speech along with them.

To put the point in the terms we were using earlier, if our primary term becomes identical with determinacy, we will end in extracting all possible content from the account that attempts to use that term as a foundation. While we have shifted to a more abstract way of thinking than that typical of the schemes of the Milesians, we are confronted with exactly the same problem. Being, no more than water or fire, can stand alone as a fundamental term. To take its place in an orderly scheme, to be a part of "trustworthy speech and thought about the Truth," Being requires some Other in terms of which it can take on definition. Since at this level, definition itself is also in question and taken as allied to Being, that which lacks definition stands as the only Other available. Nor are we stuck with the useless notion of Otherness per se, for the ideas associated with what is other to being are at least as clear as those that Parmenides associates with Being itself. We have only to think about the path that led us to our characterization of Being in order to discover them.

The very movement that is essential to our thought about Being lends meaning and content to its boundary, and that boundary, at least in this context, seems to be one established by not-being. At first, this seems nonsensical. Isn't suggesting that something is bounded by "not-being" simply an indirect way of saying that it is not bounded? It would be of course, if *not-being* were taken to refer to some notion of absolute nothingness, since negation in this sense, if it means anything at all, refers to the utter lack of a logical position. But that is not after all what stands in contrast to Parmenides' conception of Being. Being has been defined as whatever is utterly stable and unified. The necessary other logically entailed by that definition, the other required for the definition to be maintained, is a sense of "not-being" importantly distinct from negation simpliciter. Movement and plurality define the bounds within which Parmenides' conception of Being is constrained as the indeterminate others in relation to which his highly determinate conception is marked out. And the place of these "others" in his discourse appears to be at least as fundamental as the particular understanding of Being that has emerged, since the character of being as something utterly determinate (here, univocal and unchanging) would be meaningless without the boundaries that can be provided only by the indeterminate correlates that, to use Parmenides' image, lie outside the well-rounded sphere of Being. It may be that what lies on the other side of the boundary remains rather wild and murky, but it is nonetheless a dimension of being and of thought in the absence of which Parmenides' conception of Being would dissolve into nothing.

It seems to me that Parmenides must have been aware of this problem. If the paths outlined by the goddess were really mutually exclusive, why mention the misguided alternative at all, let alone argue that one must learn all things, including the opinions of mortals who wander two-headed down the useless path of what-is-not? In fact, the recurrent claims at the beginning and end of the "trustworthy" discourse are not unlike the Socratic warning about being blinded by the sun and the necessity for a return to the cave. Confronted by the unhappy separation between the truth and what it is supposed to be the truth about, both Parmenides and Plato—in the middle dialogues—find themselves forced into recommending a vacillation between two ways of thinking, and given their equal concern for a unified account of the whole, one assumes that neither was particularly happy with such a recommendation. And in both cases, the reason for this problem is the same. Each thinker is so blinded by his commitment to the notion that the truth must have a determinate character that he neglects the obvious and crucial place of indeterminacy in his own thought. And this tendency has continued to bewitch us ever since. The mistake inherent in it can best be exposed by thinking through a particularly interesting (and puzzling) passage in Plato's later thought where this crucial issue is treated more directly than it is anywhere else that I am aware of prior to Hegel.

III. BEING, OTHERNESS, AND INDETERMINACY

a. Not-Being and Thought

As we have seen, when confronted by a choice between sameness and difference, unity and plurality, the limited and the unlimited, stability and change, Parmenides decided in favor of a univocal understanding of Being, supposing that understanding (or, more broadly, "thought") itself requires such a choice. Nor is his choice an arbitrary one. If Being is not linked to sameness, how could we establish any meaningful self-identity for it? If it is not unified, then understanding one dimension of it would not necessarily lead to understanding other dimensions. If it is unlimited, then any knowledge of it would be at best incomplete, and there would be no way to judge even the degree of its incompleteness. If it is in a state of change, all of these problems would be magnified and multiplied. Hence it seems not only reasonable but necessary to think of being as utterly immutable, internally undifferentiated, perfect and complete. The problem is that it is not at all clear that we actually can *think* of such a thing. What would this thinking be like? We can utter a string of words like "stable, unified, bounded, perfect, complete," and so on, but even these must stand apart from Being itself, since otherwise such terms could be differentiated neither from one another nor from Being. On Parmenides' view, Being is utterly undifferentiated, and given his understanding of the relationship between Being and Thought, it follows that logical differentiation is impossible. If Being is held by necessity within unshakeable bonds, so is Thought—at least so is *genuine* thought. Thought in its more ordinary and familiar sense fades away, wandering uselessly along the illicit path of what-is-not. So does virtually every other dimension of ordinary experience. There opens not just a distinction between reality and appearance, but a yawning and unbridgeable chasm. We are transfixed. To open our mouths is to tell a lie. Where can we go from here?

In his later work, particularly in the *Parmenides* and the *Sophist*, Plato examines this problem with great care, though he meets with limited success in the attempt to solve it. Both dialogues remain inconclusive even by Platonic standards and, given the breadth of the problems that they treat, that is not surprising. Interestingly, in the beginning of the *Parmenides*, Plato has Parmenides himself articulate the issue—rephrased in terms of the ontology of the middle dialogues—as he gently shows the young Socrates that positing a realm of forms does not really solve the logical problems that it is meant to handle. In fact, it leads not only to a radical separation between reality and appearance, but also makes a knowledge of the real (the forms) impossible. It is particularly important to note that the whole of this discussion[14] is driven by a basically epistemic concern, and that the preliminary conclusion that Parmenides reaches concerning the possibility of knowing the forms is based on the presupposition that they must have a definite character. Even though it leads to the apparently inevitable conclusion that the forms are unknowable, it seems to Parmenides that we must start with this assumption:

> . . . if, in view of all these difficulties and others like them, a man refuses to admit that forms of things exist or to distinguish a definite [ἕν] form in every case, he will have nothing on which to fix his thought, so long as he will not allow that each thing has a form [idea] which is always the same, and in so doing he will completely destroy the significance of all discourse.[15]

And then Parmenides asks much the same question I asked a moment ago. What are you going to do about philosophy? He suggests to Socrates that before asking questions about particular forms like the beautiful or the just, he needs a "preliminary training." What Plato presumably means in all of this, as he will show in slightly different terms in the *Sophist*, is that the logical foundations of the position of the "friends of the ideas," as he calls them in the latter dialogue, have not been adequately explored. A deeper logic must be sounded and articulated before the relatively straightforward task of delineating the relations among determinate classes can be undertaken.

As the *Parmenides* proceeds, we find Plato juxtaposing and juggling the central logical ideas of Parmenides' poem, searching for some solid ground

---

14. *Parmenides*, 130b–135c
15. Ibid., 135bff.

upon which this deeper logic might be built. It turns out that the play between being and not-being allows a curious movement that seems to make the logical structure of the poem return to call its own basic presuppositions into question as it twists back on itself. The one turns into the many, the many into the one, sameness spins into a difference that cannot maintain an identity without denying it and devolving into the same, and on and on, the logical movement spiraling in all directions, sometimes seeming entirely out of control, but always returning to a recognizable position.

The *Parmenides* is rich with important insights, tossed off almost recklessly as Plato gives this kind of logic free rein, but in the *Sophist* this careening logic is brought under control in a sober and exacting attempt to come to terms with the fundamental character of logical discourse. Here Plato introduces an anonymous Eleatic thinker who will try to make sense of the position adopted by his "father" Parmenides. Now the deeper logic can be explored in terms of the central problem faced by Parmenides: no sooner does one agree that we cannot speak about what-is-not than he has to admit that he has just done so. Nor is this to be put aside as a peculiarity of language. If it is the task of philosophy to distinguish the true from the false, the real from what is merely apparent, this distinction has to make sense. Or, again, if Plato wants to drive the sophists from the city, he must first find a way of identifying them. To try to adhere strictly to Parmenides' injunction against speaking of what-is-not would mean sacrificing all distinctions between the true and the false and, at least in practical terms, would amount to endorsing even those views that are nothing more than "semblances" of the real. (Actually, even that point has to be made negatively. Such views would not be endorsed, but neither could they be denied, and that amounts to the same thing when one is confronted by a belligerently talkative fool.)

There must be some way of making sense out of not-being, and the "pursuit" of the sophist becomes a figure for the pursuit of not-being. After various twists and turns, the Eleatic stranger chases the sophist into "the darkness of not-being where he is at home and has the knack of feeling his way."[16] Before he proceeds with his discussion, the Stranger pauses to point out that there is an interesting similarity to be drawn between the sophist and the philosopher. Just as the sophist is obscured by the murky character of his realm, so is the philosopher "difficult to see because his region is so bright."[17] It seems to me, especially in light of the discussion that is to follow, that Plato is warning us that the earlier conception of the philosopher—and of philosophy—may have to be reformed. Some of the "darkness" of the sophist's realm must be brought into the "light" of the philosopher's if we

---

16.   *Sophist*, 254aff.
17.   Ibid.

are to see either clearly.[18] Without shadows, the bright is as formless as the dark. A complicated discussion of the interplay among the major forms follows, and it is in this discussion that Plato tries to find a way around both Parmenides' problems and his own as he struggles with the relation between being and not-being.

I first had reason to work with this part of the *Sophist* several years ago while developing an argument against Hegel's reduction of negation to difference.[19] Because Hegel had himself referred to this section of the *Sophist*, it seemed a good place to begin, and Plato's discussion has stuck in my mind ever since. At that time, I was primarily interested to show that Hegel had followed Plato in eschewing a radical sense of negation in favor of a relative and mediated one, thereby laying the groundwork for the utterly comprehensive mediation that is the work of the Absolute Idea. While I am as convinced now as I was then that there is something fundamentally unsatisfactory about the Hegelian account of negation, I can now see that those concerns led me to overlook the deep significance of this passage for an understanding of an even more fundamental issue—the logic of determinacy.

By the time that Plato was working through these ideas, he must himself have wondered whether he would ever make his way out of the labyrinth of not-being. But he must also have understood that unless he could find some way of making sense of not-being, his work would hit the same roadblock that Parmenides' had. In the end, he found a way of making a place for the concept of not-being within the region of intelligible discourse, but I think that he neglected some of the logical ramifications of having done so, as in one way or another, we have continued to do ever since. All of this revolves around the very peculiar logical character of "the other" and the crucial role it plays in the logical framework that Plato developed as a way out of the labyrinth. Since it is also within this framework that the logical foundation of determinacy is laid open to view, it is a framework that merits the closest examination.

Having failed in his attempt to "capture the sophist" by means of ordinary classes and categories, the Stranger decides to try to narrow his focus to include only those classes essential to any logical discourse. First then, there must be some term that refers to what-is, Being. Next, in a relatively short passage, the Stranger radically modifies the position of the "friends of the forms" (Plato's middle position as articulated in the *Phaedo, Republic,* etc.), arguing that change must be real. Otherwise, knowing and being

---

18.   The same point is made at 250e5, but put directly in terms of the relationship between being and not-being: "Since being and not-being participate equally in the aporia, there is now some hope that as either emerges more dimly or more clearly, so will the other."

19.   *Individuals and Individuality*, pp. 33ff.

known would be completely divorced from reality; the forms would remain altogether inaccessible to the soul. And yet, it is to just such a conclusion that Parmenides' strict logic—recovered and given a slightly different shape by the friends of the forms—appears to lead. Finally, the Stranger, sounding as exasperated as Plato himself must have felt, blurts out, "But tell me, in heaven's name, are we really to be so easily convinced that change, life, soul, understanding, have no place in what is entirely [παντελῶς] real—that it has neither life nor thought, but stands immutable in solemn aloofness, devoid of intelligence?"[20] Theatetus agrees that that would be a strange doctrine to accept indeed.

It is not only a strange doctrine, it is a logically futile one. It leads nowhere more surely than the trail of the sophist does, since we find ourselves very quickly encumbered with an assortment of barren logical concepts: determinacy per se, otherness in itself, 'changelessness' independent of change. At this juncture in the *Sophist*, Plato doesn't bother to produce any argument against such a view, but dismisses it out of hand as obviously untenable. Hence "we must admit that what moves and motion itself are real things."[21] And another major class, *motion*, is added to the list begun with *being*. This immediately calls up a third. While he is ready to insist that motion must be introduced into the list of those things that are fundamentally real, the Stranger also argues that if everything were in motion, we would be unable to think, since nothing would remain sufficiently constant to be cognizable. *Rest*, then, has to be added to *being* and *motion* to form a triad. Now the Stranger has already parted ways with his father Parmenides, of course, but as yet, has produced no argument to show that such a departure is logically acceptable. After all, it is one thing to be exasperated at a logical impasse and quite another to show that one can get around it. In his treatment of the remaining two "major classes" and the play that they introduce into an understanding of the first three, Plato tries to show that there is an acceptable solution to the problem of introducing not-being into logical discourse at least far enough to allow for distinctions between the true and the false. Very quickly now, sameness and otherness take their places in the scheme. Sameness is needed in order to account for the self-identity of the first three classes in a fairly obvious way, and in a much more curious way, otherness turns out to be necessary for exactly the same reason.

Being, motion, and *rest.* If we are to treat these as "classes" or "kinds" at all, we have to think of each as in some sense excluding the others. But the "exclusion" that is called into play here is already qualified, since it is prima facie evident that *being* must participate in the definition of *motion* and *rest* if the latter two are to have any meaning whatever. While perhaps not as im-

---

20.   *Sophist*, 249a.
21.   Ibid., 249b.

mediately obvious, the same thing applies even to the relation between *motion* and *rest*. These two are reciprocally bound to one another, since any attempt to define the one inevitably requires the other. But, in the midst of this reciprocal interweaving, each of the three classes maintains an insistent self-identity that holds it apart from the others as something for itself. The logical ground for that self-identity must be accounted for by a term that is not itself identical with any of the first three (since if it were identical with one of them, the other two would lose their individual identities), and the *same* (or *sameness*) is introduced to provide this ground. Now Plato has to show that these first four classes can be at once separate and interrelated. This may not at first seem particularly difficult. But the logical character of the interrelations makes the issue a rather complex one. Each of the classes must maintain its own separate identity to prevent any one from so dominating the others as to cause a collapse into a single term. At the same time, none of the fundamental terms can be treated as *wholly* separate from the others, since each depends upon one or more of the others for its own definition. *Being* must somehow enter into *rest* if we are to say that *rest* exists; *rest* requires *motion* to provide the logical boundaries necessary to its own definition; *sameness* must enter into the character of each of the others to secure their independent identities, and so on. But it now becomes clear that another logical term is needed to provide a ground for the curious blend of independence and collaboration that has developed within the framework. It may be that *motion* is logically required by *rest*, but it is required as an *other*. Equally, *being* must enter into each of the other terms if they are to be meaningful, but they remain *other* terms. Even *sameness*, while it was first introduced as a term to describe the self-reflexive character of the internal definitions of the other terms, must maintain an identity of its own that is distinctly *other* with respect to them, since if it did not, it would only serve to undercut the very character it is meant to establish. (The others would dissolve into a barren and indiscernible sameness.) Hence, a fifth term, the *other* (or *otherness*), is designated to complete the logical profile of the relations that bind and separate the first four.

As I mentioned, I have been thinking about this passage for some time. When I first looked at it carefully, my interest in it was confined to its place as the tradition's first genuinely self-conscious treatment of negation. I was arguing in favor of radical opposition for purposes only peripherally related to the present discussion, and my attention then was so much directed toward a defense of immediacy as against ultimate mediation that I neglected one of the most interesting features of Plato's analysis. Deeply entangled in the convolutions of Hegel's logic, I attended only to that part of Plato's logic that seemed to provide Hegel with the devices necessary to set the stage for the ultimate hegemony of Spirit. And, I continue to think that Plato does just that. But it is not only by developing the sense of negation that Hegel would use to try to transform the radical negation of Being and Nothing into the domesticated difference of Determinate Being. The notion of "relative not-being" that emerges from the *Sophist,* the notion that Hegel uses from first to last to show that difference is overwhelmed by sameness in the overarching unity of the Absolute Idea, becomes viable directly as a result of Plato's treatment of *sameness* and *otherness* as fundamental logical categories. These two notions are turned into classes as the Stranger's argument proceeds, and while there is some recognition that they are rather odd classes, no close examination of their own "sameness" and "otherness" with respect to the first three classes is offered.

In Plato's account, *otherness* is set apart from the first four terms as one that must always be *relative* to some other. Whereas the first four partake of *sameness, otherness* cannot, since that would entail the unacceptable consequence that there be some instance—which, in this context, is as much as to say some "understanding"—of otherness that was *not* other. Or, *otherness,* in order to be what it is, can never take on a simple and self-identical meaning. It is not possible to conceive of otherness in itself or absolute otherness. This can also be said of each of the other four terms, but not for the same reason. That is, we might move toward various and equally undesirable logical ends by positing one of the others as an absolute, but we would not immediately contradict ourselves. *Otherness* is utterly, fundamentally, even self-reflexively, *relative.* This at first seems trivially true, inasmuch as otherness is in one sense nothing more than a name for a certain relation. It becomes more interesting, however, when it turns out that this character that otherness contributes to the scheme develops into a pervasive one. Each of the first four classes, in partaking of *otherness,* also becomes relative. In the Stranger's words, "we shall say that this nature pervades all the forms, for each one is other than the rest, not by virtue of its own nature—[i.e., by virtue of its relation to *sameness*]—but because it partakes of the character of otherness."[22] In the case of *motion,* for example, it is necessary to say that it both is and is not the *same,* since it is the same as itself, but different from *sameness.* And Plato says that it is because of its combination with *otherness* that it is "not the same." Nor, as he hastens to add, is there any problem with contradiction here, since the sense in which it is "the same" is different from the sense in which it is "not the same" or *other* with reference to what it is not.

Initially, this seems straightforward enough: *motion* clearly has to be different from *rest,* and one way of expressing this is to say that it is "other" than *rest* just to the extent that it is "not rest." And of course, following the same line of reasoning, it turns out that *motion* is in a similar sense different from each of the other classes, which entails the assertion that it is different from *being.* And if that is the case, we seem forced to admit that an instance

---

22.   Ibid., 255e.

of "not-being" *is*, at least to the extent that *motion* is not *being*. That is, the form of *motion* is logically distinct from the form of *being*. What *motion* means is not the same as what *being* means, any more than it is the same as what *same* means. There has to be something then, that *motion is* that is not what *being is*. Or, "not-being" is part of what *motion* is, since to be intelligible, *motion* must maintain its difference from *rest*, and to be different from *rest*, it has to be different from *being* because *rest* also partakes of *being*. Of course, *motion* also has to be different from *sameness*, since if it were not, its own identity would be called into question—and this regardless of the fact that the concept of such an identity requires the form of *sameness*. In sum, in order for *motion*, or any other fundamental "class" to be what it is, it must "have some share of" not-being. The logical determination of each of the basic terms in the framework is made possible by the blend of position and negation that is introduced through the peculiar character of *otherness*.

This leads to a certain paradox in the case of *being*, but Plato is obliged to accept it. Since *being* is also other than the rest, the Stranger says, "being likewise is not in as many respects as there are other things, for not being those others, while it is itself, it is not all that indefinite number of other things."[23] And finally, a few lines further along, the Stranger concludes that "when we speak of not-being, it seems that we do not mean something that is the opposite of *being*, but only something that is different." And with that, it appears that logical discourse can be reconciled with not-being after all; in fact, it begins to look as though not-being, now understood as *otherness*, is a concept that we cannot do without. And it also seems that Plato has solved Parmenides' problem; at least, the dialogue proceeds from this point as though it is a problem that we can put behind us as we go on to examine other issues. In fact, Plato will argue that the very possibility of intelligible discourse requires a recognition that not-being exists and exists on an equal footing with *being*.

In part, his argument returns quite simply to its starting point. The problem that led to the ontological treatment that we have been discussing was first presented as a logical one. If it is impossible to speak intelligibly of not-being, then logical discourse itself is called into question, since there would be no ground for distinguishing the true from the false. Now, as not-being is drawn out of the darkness of the sophist's retreat into the realm of the fundamental classes to take its place as one among the others, that problem seems to be solved. There is at least a sense in which not-being *is*, and that introduces the possibility of falsity. This makes it possible to return to the divisions with which the dialogue began and to capture the sophist in a net of false images—semblances as opposed to likenesses, φαντασία vs.

---

23. Ibid., 257a.

εἰκασία—thereby distinguishing him from the philosopher, and his speech from true discourse. In short, if we can make sense of what-is-not, we can assert that it is in principle possible to identify what-is, and philosophy can proceed.

b. The Otherness of Otherness

It becomes more and more clear upon reflection that it is *otherness* that holds this whole framework together—that is, not the more obvious candidates, *being* or, perhaps, *sameness*. For it is *otherness* that makes each of the other fundamental terms identifiable in its own right as a determinate being. It might seem that this is the logical task of *sameness*, but actually, even *sameness* becomes meaningful only in contradistinction with *otherness;* and in any case, it was an overweening emphasis upon sameness that got Parmenides into the trap that Plato is trying to escape. But a certain problem arises. *Otherness* will not, after all, fit into the scheme in quite the way that the other fundamental terms do. It is crucial to the very possibility of the scheme, to what Plato calls "the weaving together of forms,"[24] since without it, there is no way of determining the character of the other four classes sufficiently to even begin to discuss their relations to one another, but it cannot itself be determined in the same fashion. Plato tries to gloss over this unhappy logical fact, but his argument just doesn't hold water. That is, he tries to turn *otherness*—now considered baldly as not-being—into one among several determinate forms:

> May we now be bold to say that not-being unquestionably *is* a thing that has a nature of its own—just as we found that the great was great and the beautiful, beautiful, so too with the not-great and the not-beautiful—and in that sense not-being also, on the same principle, both was and *is* not-being: a definite form [or, single form, εἶδος ἕν] to be counted among the many beings? Or have we any further doubts about it, Theatetus?
> None at all.[25]

There is, however, good reason to entertain some doubt about at least part of what the Stranger argues here. His reasons for trying to insist that not-being can take its place among the rest of the forms are quite clear. Having held from his earliest days that knowing something means being able to give a stable account of it, being able to tie it down, Plato is already committed to the notion that intelligibility is linked in a fundamental way to determinacy. And he continues to assume, even by the time of the *Parmenides* and

---

24. Ibid., 259e5
25. Ibid., 258b11ff.

the *Sophist*, that the forms themselves have a determinate nature, however elusive a full account of that nature might be. He may have decided to admit that the relations among the forms actually enter into their respective natures, raising some questions about the character of the boundaries that separate them, but that they have some character in themselves that remains the "same" goes—almost—without saying. But as Plato works through the logical perplexities of the *Sophist*, trying to solve Parmenides' problem and his own, he finds that he must introduce the rather dubious notion of *otherness* into the most fundamental level of the scheme of things. This is made necessary not only as a way of getting around the problem of not-being, but also by the prerequisite that the ultimate speech must have a determinate character. Without *otherness*, there can be no determinations; and without distinct and separable determinations, we would be stymied once again, with an undifferentiated and hence ineffable Being barring the road to any further inquiry, making impossible all distinctions—not least of them, the distinction between itself and what is not.

Otherness must be granted a place in the scheme of things, whether we want it there or not. Having admitted this much, the next move is to try to contain the notion somehow before it is allowed to call into question the very determinacy that it was introduced to establish. Unhappily, this cannot be done. At least, we cannot argue both that *otherness* is required for determinate logic and that logic is somehow in itself and fundamentally determinate. *Otherness* carries indeterminacy into the most fundamental level of our thinking, and that indeterminacy remains there, continuing to perform a crucial logical function, however insistently we choose to ignore it.

Sameness and otherness seem to enter into relations with the other major classes as similar logical structures, or Plato tries to treat them in this fashion. But when he does so, he neglects their logical origins. Both, and most obviously, otherness, actually participate in the framework first as ways of describing relations among the other classes.[26] Otherness enters into the framework at first as a name for the separate characters of the classes when considered in contradistinction with one another. It is tied to the *being* of each of the classes (including of course *being* itself) at least in the sense that none of them could be what it is without its participation in otherness.

Think again of the case of *motion*. The Stranger draws this term into the scheme as something that must be given a fundamental ontic and epistemic

---

26. While this is not quite true of sameness, inasmuch as its first task is to provide a logical foundation for the self-identity of the terms of the original triad, it becomes equally true of its larger place in the frame when it turns out that exclusion turns on itself to show a necessary relation between the terms excluded from one another. Necessary in the sense that they would remain unintelligible—unidentifiable—without it.

position if we are to avoid the problem confronted first by Parmenides and then in a modified form by the "friends of the ideas." *Motion* is what it is as *other* than *rest*. It might seem that in having said that, we have said enough to identify *motion* and to give it a place in the scheme, but further reflection shows that this is not enough. Although distinguishing *motion* from *rest* makes a start, it must also be distinguished from *being*, not only to avoid a descent into the maelstrom of an all-consuming *motion*, but also to make it possible to give *rest*, and thereby *motion* itself, an intelligible character. Whether we are considering the status of *motion* from an ontic or an epistemic point of view, in other words, its relation to what it is not is crucial to its own being and intelligibility. It must be *other* than *being* in order to *be* at all, since if *motion* were the same as *being* it would not be able to move, unless *being* qua *being* moved, and that would undercut the ontic status of *being* itself as Parmenides had shown. But, shifting now to the epistemic side of the problem, distinguishing it from *being* is clearly not enough to identify *motion* as something with a distinct meaning unless *being* were identified with *rest*, and that cannot be done without depriving *motion* of meaning. Hence *rest* enters the scheme as an *other* crucial to the epistemic status of *motion*, and by the way, as a third determination that must maintain its *otherness* from *being* for reasons both ontic and epistemic.

It is worth noting now that *sameness* cannot perform the logical function necessary here. Saying that *motion* is the same as itself, in the absence of any assertion about what it is different from, would leave us again in the Parmenidean bind by reducing motion to an empty abstraction. Equally in the case of the other two original classes, the assertion of a bald self-identity is not a useful logical move until it is combined with the logical function of *otherness*. The "weaving together of forms" to which we owe the possibility of "any discourse we can have" depends upon the series of relations established by *otherness*. Plato would like to hold that this means that *otherness*, now in the guise of "not-being," *is* in the same sense that the first four terms *are*, but its ontological character is importantly different. Where each of the others can be considered determinate beings, separable if not separate in their self-identities, this cannot be true of *otherness* itself. In fact, the problem is precisely that the term "otherness itself" does not make sense. *Otherness* may blend with each of the other forms, but that does not mean that each of them blends in a reciprocal fashion with it. Each of the other forms depends upon *otherness* for a crucial part of its own definition; there must be a meaningful "other" in order for the term in question to be intelligibly identified as "the same as itself." This, interestingly, is as much true of *sameness* as it is of *being, motion,* and *rest.* But the play between sameness and otherness that provides the ontological determination of the first four terms does not apply in the same fashion to *otherness* because it is impossible for *otherness* to be the same as anything, including itself. As a result, *otherness* cannot take on the determinate character of the rest of the terms in the scheme and remains to this extent outside the realm of determinate being. And yet, it is equally *inside* this realm as the relation that sustains the onto-logical distinctions that make it possible to treat the other primary terms as determinate.

It may seem that the term *determinate being* has leapt unannounced into our discussion. But it is actually determinate being that has been under con-sideration from the outset. As soon as Plato distinguishes *being* from *motion* and *rest*—or as soon as it is distinguished from anything whatever—the Par-menidean sense of Being has been left behind. And it is left behind because it must be if logical discourse is to develop. It is no more possible to say anything of Absolute Being than it is to speak of Absolute Nothingness. In the absence of any other meaningful concept, the notion of Absolute Being is lost in a logical waste every bit as trackless as that into which Absolute Nothingness disappears. (So far the Hegelian analysis is right.) If we are to proceed at all, we must create a path, and we can do so only by introducing the possibility of differentiation into this most fundamental level of our thought. It was not unreasonable to suppose that univocity has some prior claim on the nature of what is, but it turns out that univocity itself requires plurality as an ontological *other* if it is to be intelligibly attributed to anything, including *being*.

Hence in the groundwork that Plato develops in the *Sophist, motion* must be drawn into play with *being* not only to make a place for "life and thought," as the Stranger said at the outset, but also to open a logical path to the investigation of *being* itself. *Motion* carries *rest* along with it into the scheme of things as its logically necessary *other*, at the same time distinguish-ing *rest* from *being* since an identification of the two would deny the mean-ingful existence of *motion*. Once *motion* and *rest* are introduced, it becomes possible to speak of being in contradistinction with them, and that speech generates the notions of *sameness* and *otherness* as ways of describing the re-lations among the first three. Each of the first three is something distinct from the others and hence self-identical. In being the *same* as itself, each is *other* than the rest, and a pathway is opened to logical discourse about de-terminate being.

At first, there seems nothing particularly striking in the fact that Plato treats *sameness* before dealing with *otherness*. We are so much in the habit of giving *sameness* pride of place that it seems natural to introduce *otherness* as the fifth and last of the "comprehensive classes" and then to go on to a dis-cussion of the relations among them as if each occupies a similar position in the scheme of relations that will ultimately make sense of the concept of "not-being" and apparently solve the problem with which the discussion be-gan. In fact, that is just what Plato does, even, as we have seen, going so far as to suggest that "not-being" has a nature of its own in the same sense that the other comprehensive terms have, and daring anyone to show that this is not the case. But something important is neglected in this treatment of the notions of *sameness* and *otherness*. For one thing, the position of *otherness* in this discussion must be logically coincidental with that of *sameness*. We cannot meaningfully describe any of the first three terms as the "same as itself" without reference to the others qua *others*. Each is the same as itself *by virtue of* its *otherness* with respect to the remaining two. *Otherness* enters into the scheme along with *sameness* as a logical relation without which the determinacy to which *sameness* refers would be ineffable and hence impossible. Again, this seems an unremarkable point so long as we trick ourselves into thinking of *otherness* as simply another determination among the several already introduced. And perhaps this is why Plato is at such pains to show that *otherness* considered as "not-being" or, more particularly, as the "not-beautiful," the "not-great," or the "not-just" has the same character as its positively determined counterparts. But of course it does not have the same character at all. If *otherness* has a "nature," it is to be neither a this nor a that, never determined, never even self-reflexively defined: its nature is to be indeterminate. Now since determinacy, as it is ordinarily understood, depends upon a meaningful sense of *sameness*, and *sameness* requires a meaningful—and irreducible—*otherness* for its own logical definition, then it seems that the apparently determinate framework that emerges from the interplay among *being*, *motion*, and *rest* is shot through with indeterminacy.

To the extent that each of the other terms is at least partially constituted by its participation—to use the Platonic expression—in *otherness*, the fundamental logical structure of *otherness* pervades the framework not only as a description of the relations among the first four terms, but equally as an essential ingredient in the logical structure of those terms considered in themselves. The great temptation here is to suppose that, since the *other* in various particular cases seems to have a determinate character, it follows that *otherness* considered independently also has such a character. When, for example, we describe the play of *otherness* in the constitution of *motion*, we typically do so by calling up another apparently determinate term, *rest*, and end in thinking that the *other* in this case has a nature similarly determinate to that which it grants (by contradistinction) to *motion*. And, since if we started instead with *rest*, the same would follow with respect to *motion*, this seems quite reasonable. The *other*, considered along these lines, seems to have the function of a limit, and since the limiting term can in most cases itself be considered limited (as in this case *rest* is by *motion*), we begin to think that *otherness* not only functions to introduce limits, but is itself limited.

In fact, the Platonic analysis follows a line something like this. Plato certainly recognizes that *otherness* is fundamentally relative, but, as we have seen, he nonetheless goes on to argue that *otherness*, now considered as not-being, can be counted as one among the many determinate beings with a nature of its own. He moves to this conclusion from an analysis of not-being that is intended to show that it can be "cut up into small bits" just as he thinks knowledge can be. That is, not-being comes to be understood as a composite of the not-just, not-great, not-beautiful, and so forth, each of which is treated as though it clearly had some determinate content of its own. But this is to make the mistake just mentioned of supposing that because some determinate character can be attached to the *other* of this or that determination, it follows that otherness has a similar character itself. Again, in the case of motion, we immediately upon bounding it by means of its *other* call *rest* into play and imagine that we have hit upon a way of determinately characterizing *otherness* at least in this case. But there are at least two fundamental reasons for arguing that this is not the case. For one, *rest* relies upon *motion* in a reciprocal fashion for its own determination and is in this sense bound to the being of motion. But more importantly, *rest* is only a partial representation of *otherness* in respect to *motion*, since, for example, *being* must also be considered *other* in relation to *motion*. So, for that matter, must every possible determination; and if we choose to think of those determinations as a kind of list, the character of *otherness* makes it a list that can never be completed. Since *otherness* enters into the treatment of any determinate being whatever in the same fashion, we no sooner establish a determinate identity than we give rise to a logically boundless *other* without which the boundaries of determinacy cannot be established.

It is certainly the case that philosophy can proceed only by moving beyond the absolute conception of being articulated by Parmenides. In order for that movement to become possible, Being must open itself to the differentiation of determinate being since without that differentiation no second moment or form could be intelligible. But we find that the introduction of distinctions within being requires an intelligible conception of not-being and that conception is inexorably bound to the logical character of *otherness*. There are good reasons for having introduced rest and motion into this particular framework, but thinking simply from the perspective of the abstract requirements of logical discourse itself, it becomes clear that *some* such notion or notions would have to be introduced if we are to escape Parmenides' trap. To lay a logical foundation for determinate being, there must be some *other* from which *Being* is distinguished, and that thereby provides the limit that makes a conception of determinate being intelligible. Unfortunately, the limit is not itself limited. The character of *otherness* makes it in principle impossible to completely articulate the nature of the boundaries by which determinate being is established. This means that there is a necessarily indeterminate dimension of any determinate framework, and that we must remold and open our models of intelligibility to accommodate it.

IV. MAKING-DETERMINATE AND INDETERMINACY

Having begun this chapter with a kind of apology for the reflective remove that I was about to undertake, it seems appropriate to end it with some similarly direct comments about just where that remove has led us. I have already mentioned my reasons for having chosen the Platonic context as an appropriate one for coming to grips with the logic of determinacy. And I continue to think that this context is peculiarly appropriate in both historical and logical terms. However, given the highly technical character of the argument in the preceding sections, it seems to me that there is some danger of losing track of the chief issue at stake.

It seems obvious that Plato's choice of being, motion, and rest as primary terms in this argument was not an arbitrary one: when he refers to these three terms, along with sameness and difference, as μέγιστα γένη, he means what he says. From being, motion, and rest, after all, it is possible to develop not only an abstract logical framework, but equally a physics that can be brought back to the world of direct experience as an account of the phenomena with which one began. These *are* absolutely fundamental and comprehensive categories, and they must be considered at some point by anyone who tries to develop a full-fledged account of what is. However, while they provide a reasonable and productive starting point, there is nothing necessary about beginning with them. We might choose some other starting point altogether, thinking, say, in more concretely physical terms or in more abstractly theoretical ones. But no matter where we begin, the structure of logical thought itself will drive us to the same conclusions reached earlier. The indeterminacy that has been uncovered as a necessary constituent of the apparently determinate framework of the *Sophist* obtains equally to the development of any determinate framework whatever.

If we are to move beyond the mere assertion of a first position, we must mark out intelligible boundaries that allow a consideration of that position in juxtaposition with some other. And though the other may come to take on some determinate character of its own, the play between this other and the first position can never be wholly determinate because the boundary that separates the two is not itself wholly determined by the internal structure of either the first or the second term. In fact, since those terms can be thought to have "internal structures" or "meanings" only after the boundary has been identified, it becomes all too clear that the activity of bounding cannot itself be entirely bounded and, as a result, that any attempt at making-determinate will issue in a certain indeterminacy.

Given the modern preoccupation with consciousness, we are typically disposed to attribute the appearance of indeterminacy to our own activity, as if it were mind that was throwing a wrench into the otherwise determinate works of its objects. But as we have seen in various different contexts, boundaries *themselves*, even if we try to think of them independently of *our* experience—though, frankly, I can see little point in doing so—are not bounded. At least, it is clear that they are not bounded in the sense that the terms or entities that they bound are. We struggle to understand the world and our place in it by noting various dividing lines, by "cutting it up into small bits" as Plato says, only to find that the lines of division will not stand fast, cannot themselves take on the determinate character of the "things" that they are taken to mark out. Supposing that these lines have such a character amounts to a logical mistake similar to the practical one of searching in the world for lines that correspond to those on a map. Nor does this mean that the boundaries we are considering, whether logical or practical, are any less meaningful or any less "real" than we took them to be prior to this reappraisal. It does mean, however, that we should stop wasting our time searching for that final determination, that last knot in the net that will close the weave and capture the world at last in the complete articulation of the ultimate set of categorial distinctions. The activity of making-determinate, necessary as it is to the pursuit of any goal, is irremediably bound to the logic of otherness, and as a result to the indeterminacy that the nature of otherness drives into the center of the determinate frameworks that it makes possible.

I hope that it is clear by now that I meant it when at the end of the first chapter I said that I had no intention of arguing in favor of indeterminacy at the expense of the determinate dimensions of our experience. Holding that indeterminacy has a more fundamental place in either direct or reflective experience is as logically untenable as is the more typical uncritical bias in favor of determinacy. However, it is clear that the indeterminacy that has appeared in each of the contexts we have considered, whether we are thinking of stone walls or of the most abstract reflective schemes, is an ontological dimension of our experience of the world that cannot be ignored, reduced, or wished away.

CHAPTER 4

BEGINNINGS, ENDS, AND INDETERMINACY

. . . it shows a lack of education not to know that it is necessary to seek a proof for some things but not for others. For it is altogether impossible for everything to have a proof; the process would go on indefinitely, so that even thus there would be no proof.

Aristotle, *Metaphysics*

I. MODERN BEGINNINGS

Our attempts to make sense out of things have typically and quite naturally prompted us to establish boundaries, to identify the limits within which our ontological distinctions find and maintain their meanings. Too often, while struggling to perfect our understanding by means of the categories and ideas that issue from this activity, we lose sight of the early stages of the process, stages that I have been trying to uncover in the preceding discussion. While concerning ourselves overmuch with the beginnings of projects holds out the danger of never getting anywhere, it is nonetheless very dangerous to neglect those beginnings altogether.

I think that we have been far too ready to allow ourselves to do just that, with the result that we have often found ourselves drawing conclusions that seem to have lost touch with the original purpose of philosophical reflection. We set off to try to understand the world, typically deciding what such an understanding ought to be like before we have it, and then when no such understanding appears at the end of our work, suppose that it must be the case that we simply can't understand things at all. Or that things are nothing like what we originally took them to be. Or that there really aren't any things to be understood. Or again, that there are various equally acceptable ways of understanding things and no way to choose among them, which of course boils down to supposing that we can't understand things at all. Seldom does it occur to us that we might have made an initial mistake about what an "understanding" of things ought to be like, let alone that our presuppositions concerning this could have had any important effect on the success of our project.

Now more than ever, it has become the proper task of philosophy to recover and reconsider the presuppositions that form its own foundation. But if this is one of the most important tasks of philosophy, it is also one of the most uncomfortable, since sufficient digging will always expose the rather tenuous character of some of our most fundamental notions. As Wittgenstein says in *On Certainty*, *"Am Grunde des begrundeten Glaubens liegt der unbegrundete Glaube."*[1] And now, as I consider the course of my reflection over the past few years, it seems to me that it has revolved around tracing the roots of just such an unfounded belief. Our bias in favor of determinacy, our assumption that it is possible to completely capture and confine the world of ordinary experience by means of boundaries and definitions, has precisely this character. As I have demonstrated by considering contexts both abstract and concrete, it is a mistake to suppose that knowledge can ever have a wholly determinate character. When we begin by supposing that knowledge has such a character, we inevitably end in trying to separate determinacy from its relation to indeterminacy, succeeding only in cutting it off from its ontological roots in a way that leads to a useless multiplication of barren abstractions.

Moreover, this predisposition in favor of the determinate misleads us into imagining that the world of ordinary experience must also have (at bottom) a wholly determinate character. Instead of recognizing that the definition of boundaries, the very act of making determinate, is ontologically bound to the indeterminacy of the other, we try to subdue this crucial character of the other by means of a procrustean analysis that is doomed from the start. Ignoring the place of indeterminacy in the ontological definition of the determinate, we tell ourselves that those dimensions of experience that seem to refuse a completely and exclusively determinate exposition fall into two classes: those that have yet to be fully understood, where we suppose that a full understanding will expose their fundamentally determinate character; and those that are simply illusions, where a full understanding will show us that nothing was really there in the first place. Einstein is as ready to insist on a unified field as Spinoza was to restrict the will of God; Hume as ready to discard induction as Hegel is to dismiss the concrete particularity of sense experience.

Our bias toward the determinate dimensions of experience runs deep in Western thought. Having sought the roots of this bias as it developed in the earliest stages of the tradition, I should like to end with some comments

---

1. "At the foundation of well-founded belief lies unfounded belief." Wittgenstein, *On Certainty*, (New York: Harper & Row, 1972), p. 253.

about how the same bias has continued to play a crucial role in the development of the modern tradition. Here again, a focus on the beginning is critical, and the ancient bias in favor of determinacy shows up strikingly at the outset of the modern period in Descartes's insistence on certainty as a primary criterion for knowledge. Struggling once again to mark out boundaries, once again to discover some underlying order in the play of appearances, a new standard is identified. Certainty, the ultimate coalescence of the clear and the distinct, the closed circle of mathematical definition, will serve now as both guide and goal. Descartes speaks for his own age and for centuries to come when he begins his "search after truth" having already embraced this criterion:

> But inasmuch as reason already persuades me that I ought no less carefully withhold my assent from matters which are not entirely certain and indubitable than from those which appear to me manifestly to be false, if I am to find in each one some reason to doubt, this will suffice to justify my rejecting the whole.[2]

Reason itself is taken to demand that the standard of certainty be imposed as Descartes investigates the world and his ideas about it in search of some new and more solid foundation for knowledge. And, at least on the face of it, his claim seems reasonable enough. The notion of starting off with some assertion or set of assertions about which one can be quite sure appears to be good practical advice. But that, as Descartes finds to his dismay, is just the problem. This may sound like a practical suggestion, but as it is drawn into an examination of the sorts of things that we typically think and say about the world of practical experience, it turns out that few if any of them quite come up to the mark. Discarding what he considered to be the useless abstractions of the Schools to return to the "book of the world," Descartes actually initiates a way of thinking that will lead to an even more radical break between reflective and direct experience than the view that he was anxious to leave behind.

In focusing on Descartes's beginning, I do not intend to try to offer some new insight into what Descartes himself intended. His ideas are rather of interest as a firm and formal articulation of the ontology of modern philosophy. I mean to use the word *ontology* here in the sense that I have been using it throughout, to refer to the fundamental play between ontic and epistemic concepts and commitments that serves as the ground for the systematic or categorial claims that are drawn explicitly into the development of

---

2. *The Philosophical Works of Descartes*, ed. E. S. Haldane and G. R. T. Ross (Cambridge: Cambridge University Press, 1931), p. 145.

our thinking. And the ground-level commitments that come together to form Descartes's ontology are interesting not only in themselves, but as the foundation for the tradition that he initiates. Although Descartes represents himself as beginning his project without prejudice, he is in fact already committed to a particular view of reason and understanding that will inform and direct his project as it develops away from this beginning. In both the *Meditations* and the *Discourse*, he seems to be starting with the concrete world of ordinary experience and with the kinds of claims that have the character of what he calls "moral" certainty. However, in both cases, the way that he proceeds away from his starting point is guided by a commitment to a different kind of certainty.

It is the *metaphysically* certain that stands not only as his ultimate goal, but also as the criterion against which even his method itself is to be judged. Since the kind of reflection that he will undertake is in his view saved from radical skepticism by the hope that some unshakeable truth lies at the end of the path, every step that he takes along the way is informed by that hope and by the epistemic criterion that it presupposes. This is sometimes put negatively, in the sense that he will suggest that he may find only that nothing is certain, but even that suggestion is actually made in terms of metaphysical, not moral, certainty. Upon arriving at such a conclusion, he seems to be imagining that the universal doubt such a view would entail would not itself be dubious. In any case, as we all know, Descartes is convinced well before he says any of this that at least one thing *is* metaphysically certain, and that the truth expressed in the *cogito* will maintain just the unshakeable character that his ultimate criterion requires of it.

I do not at present want to enter into the debate about whether the *cogito* actually has such a character. It is rather to the consequences of Descartes's commitment to the criterion of metaphysical certainty that I mean to draw attention. Descartes in fact moves away from the apparent starting place of the *Meditations*, away from the ordinary "certainties" of direct experience, well before he explicitly calls those certainties into question. As soon as he does so, a new relation is established, though it is one that will never figure explicitly in the development of his thought thereafter. This is the relation between the "moral" certainty of the truths that he begins by examining and the "metaphysical" certainty of the truths that he hopes to uncover and articulate. The very possibility of calling the certainties of direct experience into question depends on already having another understanding of certainty up his sleeve. It is against this other understanding that he must be judging the certainties of direct experience, since without it, there could arise no question of their being dubious in the first place. In fact, it is *doubt* that makes both kinds of certainty intelligible as logical notions, since it is in terms of doubt that they are defined. Moreover, the relation between the two kinds of certainty, a relation on which each depends for its distinct meaning, also hinges on an understanding of what Descartes means by doubt.

Doubt is the critical term here. What does it mean to call those ordinary "certainties" into question? What is the point in doing so? In one sense, Descartes' answer is fairly straightforward. He clearly hopes to be able to establish the certainty of at least some of those beliefs in a way that will stand the test of the most rigorous examination. It is not enough to assume that the floor will not suddenly dissolve beneath my feet, I should be able to demonstrate that this is the case with utter certainty. At least, such a demonstration is required if I am legitimately to claim to "know" that it is the case and then proceed to integrate it into the groundwork of a "firm and permanent structure in the sciences."[3] My belief about the floor, together with the host of similar beliefs about the world and my place in it, must be examined to see if there is any "reason" to doubt them.

Descartes's ontological commitments become more clear as we begin to learn what will count as such a "reason." Descartes, I imagine, would argue that this is the sort of thing illuminated by the "natural light" that he likes to invoke, but it does not seem to me to be quite so obvious. In fact, when it comes down to it, he is driven to some rather outlandish suggestions in order to supply "reasons" for doubt. In Chapter Two, when thinking about indeterminacy in direct experience, I alluded to the typical response of students to Descartes's suggestions, and I think that it is a response that should perhaps be considered more carefully than it usually is. The possibility that he is dreaming, the hypothesis of the evil demon, are neither of them particularly convincing when presented to people who are first reading and thinking about philosophy. In the classroom, one is anxious to direct the student's attention away from the peculiar nature of Descartes's hypotheses to focus on what is ordinarily presented as a straightforward logical point about sense information. Since virtually all of our claims concerning ordinary experience are in one way or another based on sense information, and since it is evident on reflection that sense information is sometimes deceptive, it follows that it is at least logically possible that any and all such claims may be false. Moreover, without positing an independent criterion, there is no way to establish which are true and which are false since sense information cannot provide the grounds for its own validity. And on we go to the second Meditation, hoping for better luck.

The point that Descartes is making in the first Meditation can be formulated in a number of different ways, and I do not mean to insist that the formulation I have just suggested is the best, let alone the only possibility.

---

3. Descartes, *Meditations*, ibid., p. 144.

But no matter how it is put, Descartes's point is a *logical* point. He may start off with the concrete image of a man retiring from the world to reflect at leisure on his ordinary assumptions about the things around him, but his reflection is informed from start to finish by his commitment to a highly abstract standard. In fact, the whole image of retiring from the world is clearly intended to highlight this commitment. By the time he finishes the first meditation, he is prepared to make a comment about the world of direct experience that really has little to do with that world. In the course of ordinary daily life, we do not after all have any reason to wonder whether we might be dreaming. Much less does there seem to be any reason to suppose the existence of a being bent on deceiving us at every turn. Both of these hypotheses are possible in the logical sense. Neither is likely in *any* sense. No, one says to the puzzled student, Descartes doesn't believe in an evil demon any more than you do: his point is that . . .

It is too easy to neglect the distinction between the kind of point that Descartes is making and the kind of experience to which he thinks it pertains. The doubt that has appeared by the end of the first meditation is not a doubt that arises from ordinary experience at all; it is a doubt defined in terms of metaphysical certainty. The beliefs that provide the basis for direct experience have not been shown to be open to doubt in terms of that experience, but in terms of a reflective experience that has long since departed from the concrete concerns of human practice. The "reasons" for this doubt have little or nothing to do with the practical experience they supposedly call into question. They are simply part of the abstract conception of what it would be like to be utterly certain; they are doubts that become meaningful only in relation to such a conception, to the concept of metaphysical certainty.

It is of course true that we occasionally have reason to doubt sense information, and that there is nothing particularly outlandish about pointing out that the senses can and do deceive us from time to time. But the fact that they periodically deceive us is entirely overwhelmed by the fact that, deceptive or no, we can't do without them, and we know perfectly well that we will continue to depend on them as soon as we stop doing philosophy and return to the concerns of daily life. Thinking again of the sort of discussion of this issue that one has in the classroom, it is always easy enough to multiply examples of cases where the senses deceive us, but it is much harder to think of any case where we imagine that we could be consistently and undetectably deceived. That is not to suggest that there could be no such case, but it does take rather a stretch of the imagination to think of one. Usually, it is only with distant perceptual objects that deception of this sort seems at all likely. It is quite possible to imagine being consistently deceived with respect to the physical nature of the sun, say, or of the stars. We like to think that we have those particular objects pretty well defined now, and have to consider some earlier and less sophisticated versions of ourselves to make these examples work, but there are after all similar cases in our own experience—black holes, quasars, and so on.

Still, there is always something unconvincing in these examples, since it seems as much as anything to be the distance that is causing the problem, not the senses. Once we find a way of closing the physical gap between ourselves and the object in question, it seems that the problem dissolves, and it begins to appear that it was only the distance that presented the problem in the first place. Isn't this after all what happens in our experience of the objects at our feet? One looks down as he walks along some unfamiliar path, and stoops to inspect an unusual rock or plant to make sure that it really is what it appeared to be at first glance. As we continue to reflect on our ordinary experience, there seems good reason to suppose that distance alone might explain whatever problem there is with sense information, and let it go at that: find ways to conquer distance and you will at the same time resolve the problem with sense information. None of this means that we should ignore the fact that the senses deceive us, or that we should not try to come up with ways to guard against such deception. But common sense tells us that we can usually do so simply by testing one sense by means of another. If you have reason to think that your eyes are deceiving you, use your hands, or, since in most cases even that would seem to be going to extremes, take another look.

Unhappily, while this way of getting round the problem might seem attractive from the perspective of ordinary experience, Descartes would argue, and justly, that it begs the logical question. If there is reason to doubt the senses in the first place, then any further use of them, regardless of whether the object in question is near or distant, remains open to question until some separate criterion is established by means of which the senses can themselves be tested. But the fundamental notion that such a criterion exists or should be introduced is something that Descartes treats as immune from the kind of examination to which he exposes the beliefs of sense experience. It is here that a gap opens between the logical point that he wants to make and the experience out of which it purportedly arises, and it is a gap that opens directly as a result of a misunderstanding of the relation between the determinate character of the standard that he would like to impose and the indeterminate experience against which that standard is originally defined.

Think again of Descartes's distinction between "moral" and "metaphysical" certainty. By *moral certainty*, he means to refer to our assurance with respect to beliefs of the kind that I was considering a moment ago, the beliefs of ordinary experience that are so deeply embedded in our direct action in the world that we rarely if ever call them into question. In fact, calling Wittgenstein to mind again, they are so completely a part of the way that we think about and respond to the world that it is not clear that they should be referred to as "beliefs" at all. At least, when we do refer to them in this fashion, it always seems sensible to try to separate them from the sort of claim that we would more typically characterize as a "belief." I do not ever say to myself "I believe that the floor will not dissolve" or "I believe that the sea will not suddenly evaporate." I do not think, let alone say, "I believe that the world will maintain the physical character that it has always had." I simply act on these assumptions, never so much as considering the possibility that they might turn out to be mistaken.

These are the things of which Descartes says we have a "moral assurance . . . such that it seems that it would be extravagant in us to doubt them."[4] But in the same sentence, he goes on to say that no one can deny that these same beliefs, when exposed to the criterion of "metaphysical certainty," must be considered dubious. And there is a sense in which his point is undebatable. It is true that these things about which we feel sure, "possessing a body, and that there are stars and an earth and so on,"[5] are not certain in any absolute sense. But another sort of question must be asked here. Why should we insist that these beliefs be measured against such a criterion in the first place? What would be gained by being sure beyond any possible doubt that one has a body, say? What is it that I learn when I discover, whether in an introductory philosophy classroom or simply as the result of my own reflection, that I can't really be absolutely sure about this?

Descartes wants to hold that I have learned something about what I do and do not know. He assumes that this distinction between what I know with metaphysical certainty and what I simply accept without such a test amounts to a distinction between what is truly known and what is not. The new science is to be founded on this distinction, and since we can arrive at certainty only through the understanding, another distinction turns out to be already implied by the first. In the passage leading up to the distinction between moral and metaphysical certainty, he says:

> And it seems to me that those who desire to make use of their imagination in order to understand these ideas [of God and the soul], act in the same way as if, to hear sounds or smell odors, they should wish to make use of their eyes: excepting that there is indeed this difference, that the sense of sight does not give us less assurance of the truth of its objects, than do those of scent or of hearing, while neither our imagination nor our senses can ever assure us of anything, if our understanding does not intervene.[6]

---

4.   Descartes, *Discourse on Method*, ibid., p. 104.
5.   Ibid.
6.   Ibid.

It is in the terms of the understanding that the truth is to be discovered and articulated, and this means that anything that resists the clear and distinct definition demanded by the understanding will be relegated to a subordinate position in the general scheme of knowledge—if it can be understood to have the status of knowledge at all. That about which we have only moral certainty must be characterized as "obscure and confused" in some measure and, as a result, treated as something that requires further clarification and definition before it can be brought into the precise and genuinely certain schemata that will provide the foundation for the new science.

Before Descartes's project ever really gets underway, lines of division have been drawn that will develop into the chief philosophical problems of the modern period. Where metaphysical certainty originally came into view as a logical concept defined *in relation to* the "moral" certainty of direct experience, it is now sundered from its logical ground in that relationship and taken as something that can stand on its own, purportedly maintaining a logical status not only independent of but superior to that of the concept in relation to which it was conceived and the experience that it was intended to clarify.

II. DETERMINACY AND DICHOTOMIES

As we follow the modern path, a path supposedly illuminated by Reason through the murky ground of ordinary experience, something important is left behind. This is a path that we have followed before, lifting ourselves in Parmenides' chariot to the realm of the goddess, or ascending the Platonic line by leaping from the level of πίστις to that of διανοία. The perspective from those ancient heights is as skewed as the view provided by the light of Descartes's Reason. In each case, we have been too much inclined to neglect the point from which we began, or too ready to reassess it in the light of our new perspective, imagining as we do so that we are discovering some truth that was there to be known all along. This is the fundamental point I have been trying to drive home from the earliest stages of this project in the arguments of *Individuals and Individuality*.

We cannot afford to neglect the character of the beginning in its own terms. When we do, usually by allowing ourselves to be blinded by our eagerness to reach some particular sort of end, the discontinuity between the beginning and end of our project is inevitably mirrored in the character of our accounts. Dichotomies appear at the foundation of our accounts that in the end cause more problems than they solve; gaps open that turn out to be very difficult to close. The true is separated from the apparent, forms from phenomena, individuals from universals, subjects from objects; and in each case, instead of recognizing that the relation between the terms in question

is crucial to the meaning of each, we begin to treat them separately, supposing that we have identified some irremediable fissure in the ground of
being and thought.

Time and again, such dichotomies have confounded our thought, but
rarely have we bothered to explore the logical groundwork of these apparently irreconcilable dyads. We have been much more ready to reconcile ourselves to the irreconcilable, supposing that we are driven to accept a
fundamental rift in Being itself. But these alleged gaps in being or thought
amount to nothing more than the playing out of a methodological neglect of
the relation between beginnings and ends. We return to the beginning seeking confirmation of our conclusions and reform the beginning in light of
those conclusions until the confirmation that we sought is found. The fact
that we have reinterpreted and reformed the beginning is usually lost in this
process, as we suppose along with Hegel that the "wisdom" acquired at the
end of the process affords a more complete understanding of the beginning,
rather than a merely different one.[7]

And, however unhappy the consequences, this mistake is easily explained, since it is typically the unformed and indistinct character of the beginning that we were trying to resolve, just that lack of clarity and precision
that generated the original impetus for our struggle to understand. Certainly, this is how Descartes saw his own beginning, and as the modern quest
for a new understanding begins to take shape in the development of his
thought, we find once again that hunger for definition, for some way to draw
limits around the unlimited, to discover order within chaos. But when we
think of the beginning as indistinct, or unformed, or imprecise, we are already thinking from the perspective of the end, using our own ambitions and
preconceptions as the marks against which the beginning is to be judged. To
be sure, the search for definition and structure is a natural and necessary
one, and it is easy to sympathize with Descartes when he first identifies
metaphysical certainty as the highest goal of this search and then decides to
use it as the standard against which the search itself will be measured. Nonetheless, with this decision, a peculiar tension between the goal that is chosen
and the character of the original choice enters into the very core of modern
thought.

While reconsidering the consequences of this tension, I found myself
thinking of the passage in the *Discourse* where Descartes describes the "code

---

7.   Here and later in the last section of this chapter, I mean to refer to the
central argument of the second chapter of *Individuals and Individuality*. As I argue
there, this is a mistake that leads to a serious incompleteness in the most complete
of modern systems. As a result of his neglect of this relationship, there is no place in
Hegel's system for the very form of negation required to drive the development of
dialectical logic.

of morals" that he had decided to follow. The second maxim of this code was to be "firm and resolute" in his actions, choosing a direction and following it unswervingly. He suggests that this is a good policy even when the direction is itself rather dubious, as travelers lost in the woods would be well advised to "continue to walk as straight as they can in one direction, not diverging for any slight reason, even though it was chance alone that first determined them in their choice."[8] While they may not end up exactly where they want to be, Descartes says, they will at least be better off than they were in the middle of the forest.

Descartes's commitment to metaphysical certainty has something of this character. It amounts to a choice of direction, and curiously, although the direction is defined by contrast with doubt, the original choice of direction cannot itself be free of doubt. There is an important irony here. Descartes's commitment to metaphysical certainty runs deep, but it is a commitment that has the character (at most) of a moral certainty, not a metaphysical one, since there is no way of showing at the beginning of the path that metaphysical certainty will get him out of the woods at all, let alone to the place he hopes to reach. But once having chosen his path, he follows his own recommendation, "not diverging in any direction," never stopping to wonder about the character of his original choice.

As sensible a bit of practical advice as Descartes's resolution may be in some situations, there is good reason to wonder about applying it as a universal principle. There is not much to be said for being lost in the woods, but neither is there much to be gained by getting out of the woods only to find that you still don't know where you are. It seems to me that Descartes finds himself in just such a fix at the end of the second Meditation. In fact, I think that the path he takes in the *Meditations* actually comes to a halt here, and while the arguments of the remaining four meditations are important and interesting, the split between thinking being and extended being, between the subject and the object, between Descartes's mind and whatever else there is—in short, the Cartesian brand of dualism that is destined to trouble the whole of the modern tradition—is already irrevocably established by the end of the second Meditation.

It is possible at this point to respond in the way that Descartes himself does. We might suppose that we have discovered a fundamental gap in the general structure of things and hope that some deus ex machina will appear to patch things back together again. Or, of course, we can simply choose to accept this view as an accurate description of the way things are and proceed from there in one of the directions that the tradition has in fact taken. Accepting Descartes's ontological commitments as givens, and along with them

---

8.   *Discourse*, ibid., p. 96.

the rent that they introduce into the fabric of being, the tradition divides into opposing camps each of which finds itself challenged by a dichotomy every bit as troublesome as the one that confronted Parmenides and Plato.

The knower is separated from the known, and so-called subjects and objects, consciousness and the world fall apart into what cannot even be considered halves of the same whole, since by definition only one side of the whole is available to us. Objects are reinterpreted in terms of subjects, subjects in terms of objects; the side of the knower develops into the ever larger and more complex systems of rationalism, the side of the known (or unknown, depending on how strictly we apply the Cartesian standard), into the investigations of the empiricists. Carried to extremes, the one side expands the Cartesian ego until it takes on the mammoth all-engorging shape of Absolute Spirit, while the other devolves into an increasingly narrow conception of what can be known until the wealth and splendour of the world as we experience it is reduced to the ontic deserts of logical positivism. However disparate the researches and conclusions of the two faces of the modern tradition, they share an uncritical acceptance of Descartes's prejudices concerning the fundamental character of reason and knowledge. Moreover, those prejudices drive Descartes and the tradition that follows him to suppose that we must accept a fundamental separation between thought and the world of practical experience, the very world that our thought is intended to describe and elucidate.

But there is nothing in Reason itself that demands the perfect definition, the utter determinacy, of metaphysical certainty. Far from it, in fact, our ordinary experience—which can scarcely be characterized as irrational for all its ordinariness—leads us away from rather than toward such an assumption. As Descartes himself notes in laying out his own practical plan of action, there are many times when, if we were to wait for utter certainty about our course, we should never make any progress at all. It is often necessary to plunge in, learning as much as we can, but finally acting without anything like complete knowledge. In most practical settings, it is not clear what "complete knowledge" would amount to even if we were silly enough to try to acquire it before making a decision. When Descartes insists on measuring ordinary experience against the standard of absolute certainty, he foreordains a gap between the things that meet this standard and most of what he will find in ordinary experience. And the further he goes, the more dramatic the rent in the fabric of his experience becomes, until finally there seems to be an unbridgeable chasm separating him from a knowledge of anything whatever—save an impoverished and cramped version of himself qua thinking thing.

Then begins the struggle to return to the world from which he began, but of course, since he maintains the commitment that got him into this dilemma in the first place, it is a struggle that he is doomed to lose. Even if he could prove the existence of God with the sort of certainty that he demands of himself, there would still be nothing in such a proof to provide a bridge to the world of sense experience. Either you begin by illegitimately invoking that world, as he does in the case of the third Meditation, or by divorcing yourself irremediably from it as he does in the fifth. In neither case is there any real chance of actually demonstrating that sense information can be recovered, and he is stuck with what amounts to the statement of a kind of hope in the last meditation. This is of course a rather cavalier dismissal of some difficult and extremely interesting arguments, but I am at the moment much more concerned with the origin of Descartes's problem than with his unsuccessful attempts at solving it.

The principle that he used as a guide away from the forest of uncertainty may have succeeded in getting him out of the woods, but it leaves him in a position from which further advance seems impossible—at least if the same principle is invoked as the only possible guide. I have probably pushed this little figure about as far as it will go, but I have been doing so with a reason. It is no accident that the image of a path appears over and over again in the history of philosophy. Philosophical reflection is a kind of journey, always involving a movement from one position to another and always guided by some set of principles that, once established, fade into the background as our focus is more and more directed to the ups and downs of the path that we are following. We become so involved in finding ways around the particular obstacles we meet along the way that we begin to lose track of the possibility that there might be some different solution altogether if we were to stop for a moment and consider the path from a broader point of view. We are creatures of habit, and inclined to keep to the same path unless some overwhelming reason for finding a new one presents itself.

The chief danger in this is that we begin to forget that we made the path in the first place, allowing it to begin to appear as a given. It seems to me that metaphysical certainty takes on very much this character for Descartes and the rest of the modern tradition, so that even when it leads to the logical dilemmas that we have wrestled with ever since, we accept these difficulties as if they were to be traced in the very ground of being, never thinking to look to the beginning of the path to see whether the original choice might have had something to do with the problems encountered at its end. In Descartes's case, that choice leads into the hopeless trap of the second Meditation, but he sees only the "certainty" that he has attained, and is so relieved that there was some certainty after all that he is prepared to accept the disastrous logical ramifications of locating himself in this new position. He is locked into his mind, unable even to assure himself with respect to the being of his own body, and nonetheless stays the course, never for a moment supposing that there might be something wrong with the original direction he chose. Most importantly, he seems to lose sight of the fact that he chose it.

All of the business about reason demanding this and that is an interesting way of characterizing that original choice, but it is only a way of characterizing it. Reason in itself doesn't demand anything, because its own character remains open until we decide that this will count as reasonable and that won't. While we can of course try to identify reason with absolute certainty, there is always something of reason (conceived more broadly) that lies outside the utterly certain, if it is nothing other than the character of our original choice. The move toward metaphysical certainty, however determined it may be and however strongly stated, cannot itself have the status of metaphysical certainty if for no other reason than that it is a *first* move. The sort of certainty that Descartes and his followers would like to attain is available only at the end of a path, not at its beginning. It is a certainty whose logical character requires a completing of the circle, a return that captures a beginning and transforms it into a new moment defined in terms of a whole that existed only as a possibility at the beginning.

Considered as a beginning, the choice of metaphysical certainty as a goal must carry along with it some of the indeterminacy inherent in any beginning. Or, to think about it from the point of view of other choices that might be made, it is an option picked out from among a variety of other possibilities and, as a result, an option whose meaning depends on the indeterminate array of other possibilities as the backdrop against which it will find its own definition. The path out of the woods is meaningful only if the woods are also meaningful. If we were to try to think only of the path, separating it from the context that makes it a path in the first place, we would find ourselves even more hopelessly lost than we were in the beginning, since we would thereby lose sight of the *reason* for identifying a particular direction as a path. Just as the meaning of the forest (and of our position in it) enters into the meaning of the path, so must the meaning of the experience from which we begin enter into the meaning of metaphysical certainty. However sharply defined our concept of metaphysical certainty may become when considered as a standard or goal, it also maintains something of its original character as a particular choice of direction, a choice that remains logically bound to the indefinite contours of the beginning.

Descartes's mistake is to suppose that metaphysical certainty can be extracted from the context of its original conception and treated thereafter as an independent standard. In fact, it comes to be treated as radically independent in the sense that everything else will be judged against it, but Descartes seems to lose sight of the fact that this is a reciprocal relation. Its apparent independence cannot really be maintained, since the concept of metaphysical certainty is itself defined by contrast with the dubious character of the very things that are to be judged in terms of it. Without them, that is, if we were to try to make sense of metaphysical certainty in and of itself, we would be left with another instance of the empty abstractions that we met with earlier in thinking about such notions as "determinacy per se," and so on. Because certainty is originally defined in relation to doubt, doubt also must have some place in the logical groundwork of the Cartesian account. The relation between certainty and doubt is crucial in the sense of providing the logical definition for both terms. Independently of their relation to one another, there is nothing at all, logically speaking. But once having separated the certain from the dubious, it is possible to begin to focus so single-mindedly on certainty that we lose sight of the fact that its own logical meaning continues to be tied to the dubious, that without that original distinction, the concept would mean nothing at all.

As a result, however natural our growing concern with the certain may become, it is very dangerous to lose sight of the original relation out of which the meaning of our new standard has emerged. Here, as in earlier cases, the notions are entwined in an inseparable logical bond so that in trying to extract one in order to treat it independently, we risk depriving it of its own meaning. What does it mean to be certain? The answer in the end is always that it is to be free of doubt. But for that answer to make sense, and of course that means for the question that leads to the answer to make sense, *doubt* must mean something, and, if we are to avoid question begging, its meaning cannot be defined only in terms of certainty. In other words, we must *know* what it means to be in doubt about something, and while being in doubt can sometimes be expressed by contrast with certainty, it is not always best understood in this way. In fact, since the state of being morally certain always includes doubt, there is at least one sort of knowledge that even in Descartes's own terms is specifically defined as a combination of certainty and doubt.

Before turning to a broader and more concrete discussion of these notions in the next section, it might be useful to sketch their relations in the form of the schematic ontology of the last chapter. The epistemic bias of the moderns makes it reasonable to think of knowledge instead of being as taking the fundamental position in such a scheme. (*Thought* would do just as well as a base term, but *knowledge* seems rather more appropriate to the Cartesian framework that I have been using so far.) Moral certainty and metaphysical certainty can then enter into the scheme as ontological terms that have something like the character of motion and rest in the earlier framework. Now, the point that I have been making can be put in terms of the relations among these three basic terms. If knowledge were to be strictly identified with metaphysical certainty, moral certainty would fall away as something not only separate from knowledge, but actually as something altogether meaningless, since separation from knowledge would consign it to the logical vacuum of the unintelligible. It would, in other words, cease to have a place in the scheme just to the extent that the scheme is taken to be intelligible.

Thus if moral certainty is to have any place at all, it must also partake (to use the Platonic expression) of knowledge. Moreover, since it is in terms of moral certainty that metaphysical certainty is defined, denying it a place in the scheme would mean depriving metaphysical certainty of its own logical character; and the whole business would collapse into the barren univocity of an undifferentiated first term. If knowledge is that first term, then we would be confronted with the bizarre notion of a conception of knowledge about which nothing can be said. Hence the interplay among the terms in this scheme is just as essential to their individual meanings as was that established among the "comprehensive classes" of the Platonic one. Another term also needs to be introduced as that which differentiates the two kinds of certainty, and of course, it can itself be identical with neither.

Doubt now enters the scheme as that term. While doubt is not identical with moral certainty, it participates in its logical structure as that by means of which moral certainty can be distinguished from metaphysical certainty. And since moral certainty—specifically in its dubious character—provides the boundaries for metaphysical certainty, doubt also participates, albeit in a different fashion, in the structure of metaphysical certainty. That is, without a meaningful position for doubt, there would be no way of characterizing metaphysical certainty or of going on to try to identify its relation to knowledge. Doubt plays a role in this framework similar to that of otherness in the earlier ontically biased scheme. While it cannot itself be considered limited in the determinate sense, doubt nonetheless provides the limits for the part of the scheme that will be specifically defined in terms of limitation, (i.e., metaphysical certainty and whatever part of knowledge is metaphysically certain), and thus is necessary to the logical foundation of the determinate elements of the framework. Once again, an indeterminate term is required in order to complete the logical relation on which the determinate dimensions of the scheme depend.

III. THE ORDINARY EXPERIENCE OF INDETERMINACY

While logical diagrams of the sort I have just been using are sometimes helpful, we cannot afford to depart too far from the concrete experience that they are intended to clarify. This is particularly important when the issue at hand is a return to that experience and an attempt to rethink our direct relation to the world around us. At present, I mean neither to construct more categories nor to raise technical questions about the ones that we have already conceived in our previous attempts to understand. It is the activity of understanding itself that is in question and its relation to the experience that is there to be understood. In emphasizing the importance of doubt in the Cartesian framework, I have been trying to show that while the determinate understanding that he seeks—and to a degree achieves—is a reasonable goal, it is nonetheless an end that is meaningful only in relation to its beginning. Or, it is meaningful only so long as the meaning of the beginning as it is in itself continues to provide the logical other against which the end is defined. And it is worth adding, though it seems obvious, that it is also in terms of the beginning that the end will be assessed. But this is still too abstract.

When the moderns set out on a reflective journey that is to be guided and informed by an understanding of "reason" that is itself governed by the standard of absolute certainty, they assume that what they already think about the world will be progressively transformed and clarified by means of this new standard. Well and good. But this means at least that they do already have a certain picture of the world, in fact an extremely complex and varied one, and that it is to this picture that the new standard will be applied in the hopes of a better understanding. What is unsatisfactory about the understanding that they already have? The answer, to put it in terms that will become a sort of battle cry, is that it is not sufficiently clear and distinct. We must analyze and define things, break them down into their component parts, if we are to understand them. The amorphous, the obscure, the unlimited, must be somehow tied down, confined within the limits of a determinately articulated account.

This means that there is a logical principle already being invoked and applied before the task is ever actually undertaken. Before the attempt to construct new boundaries ever gets underway, a concept that lies at its very base is established and at least tacitly defined—a particular conception of determinacy itself. We have already seen that there is no point in trying to think about determinacy per se, but that doesn't mean that it is impossible to think about determinacy as an intelligible logical structure. It just means that it cannot legitimately be conceived independently of a correlate conception of the indeterminate. When this fundamental relation is brought to bear on the project of the moderns, this means that if the new standard in accord with which the project is to develop is already biased in favor of determinacy, there must be some *other* of an indeterminate character in terms of which the determinate will be marked out and distinguished, whether as criterion, method, or ultimate goal.

One way of thinking about this *other* is in terms of the schematic characterization of the place of moral certainty and doubt in an epistemic framework of the sort just sketched. Another way of thinking about it is in terms of the world of direct experience itself. It is the room in which Descartes sits as he begins his meditations, the stove that he huddles next to as he contemplates the method that he will use, the piece of wax lying on a table waiting to be used as an instance of the insecurity of sensual experience. As we move away from that world of immediate sensation and untested convictions with Descartes, toward the careful inquiries of Locke and Hume, and toward the systematic accounts of Spinoza, Leibniz, and Newton, it is nonetheless that world that continues to stand in the background of our action and thought as our point of departure and as that against which we must finally judge whatever conclusions we reach.

Even with the articulation of what is intended to be the final system, Hegel's purportedly complete account of the Whole, still our direct experience is always there as point of departure and as final testing ground. However insistent, however intricate Hegel's attempt to completely capture the world of direct experience in his reflective net, there remains always something of it that recalcitrantly refuses the mediation and delimitation of determinately conceived categories. In *Individuals and Individuality,* I argued that Hegel leaves something behind in his attempt to speak the Whole. The relation that sustains the individual dimensions of experience, the relation that I characterized as the dyad of radical negation that undergirds our encounter with the individual both personal and otherwise, has no place in his system, and as a result the closure for which he hopes remains always out of his reach.

But now I have found that I had uncovered only a part of what is left behind, or, in his terms, *aufgehoben,* in the drive toward the Absolute. I was thinking then of particular instances of resistance, and the way they contribute to the sense of individuality that pervades our ordinary experience. Now, having thought more broadly about the general character of reflective experience, its dependence on the construction and articulation of determinate categories, and having tried to come to terms with the ensuing logical play between determinacy and indeterminacy, it has become clear that something even more important is lost as Hegel drives his system, and with it, the modern project, to completion. We have neglected the crucial sense in which the world of ordinary experience—as against our reflective appraisals of it—will always maintain the logically indeterminate character of an *other.*

In one sense, noting that the world maintains such a character is saying nothing new. From the earliest stages of Western thought, the same point has been made in countless ways. The dichotomies mentioned earlier are all of them built around the sense that the world as we immediately experience it remains somehow *different* from the world as we think it. Whether we focus on the many as opposed to the one, motion as opposed to rest, or doubt as opposed to certainty, we always seem to find ourselves confronted by the same fundamental relation that binds while it separates the one kind of experience from the other. What I have tried to bring to light is the way that the two sorts of experience are, after all, as much bound together as they are defined in contrast with one another. In fact, it is the very way that they are defined by contrast with one another that draws them inexorably together. That which appears to be univocal, at rest, to be certain, in short, the side of those pairs of contrasting terms that has always provided the foundation for our reflective schemes, from the simplest set of categorial notions to the most complete and elegant of metaphysical systems, always depends for its own definition on the other side. And while we will probably continue to try to restrict and contain the limitless depths of the other side of the relation, our attempts can never succeed since it is this very character of the other that is required for the logical structure of restriction and containment.

It will continue to be by contrast with this character of the world of ordinary experience that our categories and definitions are themselves categorized and defined. In short, the determinate dimensions of our experience will continue to be themselves defined by contrast with its indeterminate dimensions. At the most fundamental level, this appears to be a relation on which virtually everything else in our experience is hinged and to which our theories and practice always finally return. And it is the fundamentally reciprocal character of this relation that we have consistently neglected. Having established certain determinations—in the modern period, not least of them certainty itself—we depart from our own ground, and begin to use the concepts that issue from our bias in favor of the determinate as if they could stand independently of that original relation. To return to a figure from my earlier arguments, we insist on mistaking the map for the world. And that leads us into one difficulty after another. Not only does it lead to the fairly obvious mistake of intending to make claims about one kind of thing when one is in fact making claims about another; it means becoming so attached to an image that the original is finally lost through neglect or, in some cases, self-consciously discarded in favor of the image.

The "dichotomies" that appear time and again in Western thought are important examples of the sort of misconception that I have in mind. It seems to me that these dichotomies have become stumbling blocks on the path to understanding because we have misunderstood the nature of the relation that stands between the terms of the dyad in each case. Being and nothing, motion and rest, certainty and doubt—in each case, we begin to suppose that the two sides of the dyad have lives of their own, forgetting that they are only meaningful in the first place in terms of their relation to each other. The practical world in which our theories are to be tested and put to use is discarded as unworthy of our consideration since it does not come up to the mark of the standard that we earlier proposed as a way of making better sense out of it. To use the Cartesian distinction once again, we begin to reinterpret the relation between moral and metaphysical certainty. Where at first that relation was actually a reciprocal one, with each of the two terms clearly depending on the other for its meaning, their relation is so skewed as the tradition develops that we come to presuppose that if the morally certain is interesting at all, it is so only as something that may become metaphysically certain. The notion of metaphysical certainty (in one version or another) so captures the modern mind after Descartes, that we have once again turned our faces away from the world as it presents itself to us in our direct contact with it, and have redesigned our response to it in accord with the demands of presuppositions conceived independently of direct experience.

Since the original choice of metaphysical certainty as a direction (and director) was made from a practical ground, it was a choice that gained whatever meaning it had from the concrete and practical force of moral certainty. If asked at the outset about why he opted in favor of metaphysical certainty, Descartes must have responded in terms of moral certainty. He would have had to appeal to the "code of morals" of the *Discourse* or to some similarly practical guide for action. One must begin somewhere, we can imagine him saying, and given that the choice is at least at the outset an open one, why not start where one would like to end, that is, with certainty itself? If the goal of the whole program is to establish a new set of principles, principles that will in fact be distinguished as new precisely by their clarity and distinctness, by their certainty, then isn't it most reasonable to begin with certainty? And this does after all sound sensible.

But of course it is not possible. The very fact of having to ask the question makes it clear that it is not. We are confronted with various options at the beginning of the modern project, and none of them is yet clearly enough defined to demonstrate that any particular path out the woods is the best one. So we opt for what seems reasonable, what seems reasonable on at most morally certain grounds, and proceed. But the character of our beginning follows us along the path, because the path continues to be defined as much by its beginning as by its end. In logical terms, this means once again that the metaphysical certainty that defines our path continues to depend on the moral certainty with which we began for its own definition.

Even more strikingly, in practical terms, this means that each new twist and turn along the path requires the reaffirmation of our morally certain commitment to metaphysical certainty. Think of the way that Descartes himself proceeds in the *Meditations*. He stops to ask himself whether he is really to accept the apparent consequences of his decision in favor of the utterly certain. Must he really suppose that his knowledge of the piece of wax in his hand is dubious and hence to be put aside until some firmer truth exposes itself? When he decides that it is, he supposes that it is metaphysical certainty (now as criterion) that drives him to this decision. But it is actually *moral certainty* that does so. It is his practical decision at the beginning that drives him to this theoretical decision at the end. And the relation between the practical and the theoretical continues to reverberate through everything that follows, not only in the *Meditations*, but in the philosophical tradition that grows out of Descartes's ground breaking. Once again, all of this is traceable to an original choice, and to a choice that could not have had the character of the standard that has been chosen, inasmuch as it will continue to be defined by contrast with the obviously dubious character of the original choice.

Hence the separation between theory and practice that grows out of Descartes's beginning is seated in a neglect of the relation between the beginning and end of our own path. When modern philosophy finds itself confronted by an evidently irreconcilable gap between the world of direct experience and the world of reflective thought, it has already lost touch with its own ground, with the fundamental place of relations in its projects and its origin. What comes to be seen as a dichotomy is nothing more than two halves of an original whole, but a whole that does not have the character of The Whole as it is conceived by a reflective experience that attends to only one facet of the larger experience of which it is a part. The original whole is actually a relation, in this case a relation between direct experience and a reflective activity that returns to it to reshape our understanding of one beginning as it opens another. The relation between theory and practice instead of developing into what too often appears to be a dichotomy of two terms at odds with one another should instead offer new ways of thinking about still more fundamental relations, and with them, our understanding of our place in a world whose shape is constantly renewed as our ideas continue to emerge from the dynamic tension between the determinate and indeterminate dimensions of our experience.

In all of this, it is again actually the world of practical experience that maintains the character of the other against which our determinate categories and principles define themselves. Given the epistemic bias of the moderns, metaphysical certainty takes up the position of the theoretical *summum bonum* of the period, playing against the moral certainty of our ordinary experience and hence continuing to be defined in terms of the doubt that it attempts to eradicate. Now an *other* both different from and similar to that of the Platonic framework appears on the scene. The other in the guise of the indeterminate and yet fully concrete world of direct experience plays the same role as it does in the abstract schema whose intricacies we were examining in the last chapter. It is that against which the theoretical frameworks of the modern tradition are tested and refined, as it provides the fundamental relation that allows them to be defined in the first place. We reassess the ancient laws of motion, add a new and more sophisticated mathematical framework, and develop a description of our world that is thereafter tempered by the relative success of its application to the practical concerns of the human experience that gave rise to it. Theory returns to the practice from which it arose, and sometimes in the return, dramatically reforms our vision of the place from which we began. Galileo has an idea, develops an instrument to test it, and the entire concept of the center of things shifts.

Now there are other centers, around which things revolve in terms of different laws that will be given a more definite and complete form by Newton, and soon, when we look up at the night sky, we see different paths, different objects, different meanings, and most importantly, our understanding of our own relation to all of it has been radically altered. We might have been suddenly removed to a different world altogether.

But I do not want to linger over particular examples of this sort of shift in our thinking and its attendant effects on the world of practical experience.[9] For the moment I just mean to note that we live again in the midst of great change, with fundamental shifts in our thinking beginning to open new insights that may bring about changes as sweeping as those that reshaped the modern world. There is certainly a sense all around us of rebirth, of a new world awakening to a different set of challenges and to the excitement of new projects and new ways of understanding old things. But I shall put aside any more direct comment about this for the third part of my own project and speak now only of the general relation between theory and practice that has animated so much of the modern attempt to understand.

When Descartes and his contemporaries establish what will continue to be taken as the hallmark of the intelligible in the centuries that follow them, they open what has become a very familiar gap between our theoretical descriptions of the world and the world as we meet it in ordinary life. Put in starkest terms, and this is one of the reasons for having focused specifically and at some length on Descartes, this means that the world of sense experience, the world in which we are in many ways most at home, is suddenly called into question and made to appear insecure and jerrybuilt in light of criteria that are to be taken as the marks against which everything, at least everything that can be known, is to be judged. In one sense, of course, this is not a new kind of thinking at all. The ancients also wondered about the changeable character of sense experience, opted equally in favor of stability and clarity, and ended with dilemmas that if not quite the same, were nonetheless logically parallel to those of the moderns. But with the early moderns, there arises a new kind of gap. Now there is not only a split between the real and the apparent, but a split between thought and being. It is not that such a separation had never occurred to the ancients, but it was put aside as obviously doomed to lead into insuperable difficulties. (Plato, for example, dismisses the notion of separating consciousness from the world in a line or two in the *Parmenides* as something that would be hopelessly fool-

---

9. For a discussion of the kind of issue that I have in mind, see my "Mediation, Immediacy and Time," *Journal of Speculative Philosophy* 1, no. 4 (1987). The modern diremption of theory and practice and its roots in a misunderstanding of the place of indeterminacy in our conception of intelligibility will be one of the chief concerns of the third book of this trilogy.

ish.) Yet the moderns do just that, and the point to be noted is that they do so following Descartes's lead in continuing to accept certainty as a fundamental guide for thought. As a result, the new gap that opens between theory and practice carries along with it a disastrously narrow understanding of knowledge itself that is foreordained not only to maintain but to widen the gap.

So long as knowledge per se is taken to have a wholly determinate character—as any knowledge formed with the principle of certainty as guide must have—the world of ordinary experience will remain in some fundamental part removed from the categories and articulated frameworks that satisfy this demand. What is most curious here is that it is this very world of practical experience, with its vagaries and shifting contours that provides the necessary logical *other* for the establishment of the criterion that drives any knowledge based on certainty away in retreat from it. Without the formless and the unbounded, the formed and the bounded are doomed to develop into barren abstractions of the sort that we have encountered at nearly every turn in the development of our traditional ontological schemata; without an experience that is *known* as imprecise and clouded, the notion of a kind of knowledge that is clear and distinct can have no logical position or force. In fact, it is in the continual play between the two, between, for example, the highly refined theoretical goals of Descartes's project and the inevitably dubious world within which the project is taken up, that the drive and meaning, the life of the modern will to understand is established and sustained. The world continues to defeat our most concerted efforts to draw boundaries around its mysterious power, to confine its limitless sea of potential being within the determinate bays of the "new science."

Nor is this to be explained away as a function of our limited perspective. Too often have we tried to refine our charts sufficiently to bound this sea by supposing that if only we could take up a better position, if only there were some higher peak from which to observe the whole, we would see the boundaries, trace them on our larger tablet and complete the map. If only we could see as God sees, everything would come clear; and sometimes so completely enamoured of and blinded by our attempt to confine the whole, we have dared to speak from his perspective, imagining that from that exalted (albeit, of course, unattainable) view, we could prove the point and finish the speech. But this is all nonsense. And nonsense of the most fundamental sort. For it involves losing track of ourselves, forgetting that we are the makers of the map, and that no map, however carefully drawn, can include the true position of its maker. We can at most point to an image of the place from which we were drawing, and try as we might to locate ourselves there, we always remain outside it. Nonetheless, we are sometimes so taken with our image, that as in the cases we have already considered, we begin to mistake it for the original. We begin to forget that the map was intended only as a way of making our way around the world a bit more successfully and begin to think that it is itself the world or, in any case, that it offers a better and more complete understanding of it. We suppose that the world actually has those neat lines, those definite boundaries, and when the most determined search fails to uncover them, we are even prepared to suppose that there is something awry with the world. It must have these boundaries: after all they are there, clearly delineated on the map.

Now, of course, the map is an extremely useful tool, and something that as it is put into practice can actually work to reform our notion of places mapped out. We grow to think more clearly about them in relation to one another, for example, and to see parameters that are obscured by our immediate movement through the places that are charted on the image. And this is perfectly reasonable, so long as we remember that the map in our hand is at best an image of the world, and an image of our own device at that, an image formed with deliberate and unconscious biases already at play, and something that in the end cannot even itself have the wholly definite character that we would like to attribute to it and to the world that it pictures. We cannot afford to mistake the map for the world, for when we do, we run the risk of not only misunderstanding the world, but likewise of destroying the meaning of the map. The determinate boundaries that arise in the course of our attempts to make sense out of our immediate experience can lead us toward a new and better understanding of that experience only so long as we remember that they are boundaries that we have established, and that however secure they may seem for a time, they remain open to change, and even to complete dissolution.

While bringing this part of my project to a close, and beginning to work through some of the problems and questions that will be taken up in the next book, I have been walking again along the familiar paths of Inis Mór, the island that I mentioned earlier. As I was climbing a hill the other day, thinking about ends and beginnings, boundaries and otherness, I stopped to look out across the island, allowing the timeless peace of the place to wash over me for a while. It was one of those vantage points on the island from which one can see the place almost entire, and I found myself thinking again of the play between determinacy and indeterminacy in our ordinary experience of things. Here was the original of the map that hangs at home, thousands of miles away, now lying before me in its beauty and stillness. Soon, I would be back there, using the map as a reminder of this place of retreat and solitude, and perhaps thinking again of the curious relation between image and original.

From the top of the hill, the relation seems a very close one, the island looking much like a map, its boundaries clearly defined and the ubiquitous stone walls marking out distinct lines of division, separating the island into the bits and pieces of a kind of Epicurean vision of the whole. As I made my way down over the rocky outcroppings on the top of the hill, I came to a boreen, a little path bordered by two of the walls that I'd seen from the top, and followed it the rest of the way down. Now with the walls close to hand on either side, the boundaries that had been so clearly defined when viewed from the top began to wander into much less determinate shapes as the walls wound down the path, following the natural contours of the hill. The distinct divisions of the map seemed to have less and less to do with the island itself as I climbed over stones that had fallen or been knocked down from the walls. Nor had the fields on either side of the boreen anything like the geometrical definition they had seemed to have a few minutes before. Now they were small spaces that had obviously changed shape many times, and whose boundaries would continue to shift with the needs or whims of their owners.

Still in a sort of atomistic humour, it occurred to me to think of a descending order of bits and pieces, the little fields marked off by the walls themselves made out of smaller bits and so on. But as I looked at the stones at the bottom of the hill, and began to think of how they came to be there, the meanings that they had had and that they have, the true difference between the island itself and the image of a map became more and more striking. The map on my wall at home had translated itself very neatly onto the view of the island as seen from the top of the hill, but the limitations of such a view were suddenly much more interesting than the apparent similarity. I had been looking down from a place that has an ancient feel about it, one of those places that carries the ages of man with it, as I stood outside the walls of one of the ring fortresses that have stood on such promontories for millenia. These fortresses are gigantic structures, awesome in their ageless strength, but broken. The stones that had been carried up to make them by people lost in the dim reaches of the island's past, had been carried back down by others, perhaps no longer threatened in the way that the fortress builders had been, to make new things suited to new purposes of their own.

The island is alive with all the projects and hopes of its inhabitants, and small enough so that these different lives and meanings, ages and thoughts, are drawn together into a single experience that seems to vibrate and shift with each glance that one takes. The stones that formed and form the walls of those fortresses are the same stones that a later and more gentle age built into the churches and refectories and dormitories of the monks for whom the island offered a retreat for the pursuit of very different goals. Then one walks only a little further, past the remains of a round tower that might have been a part of that contemplative life, toward the remains of another building, a seventeenth century castle that housed Cromwell's troops as they kept a watch out to sea against an invasion that might override their own. But only parts of the castle remain, the stones of its walls, once so formidable and secure, now forming bits of the cottages that cluster around it.

As these thoughts wandered through my mind, the stones lost the character of determinate bits and pieces, and became instead the locus of an indeterminate being ripe with possibility, waiting to take on some new face, some unknown shape that will reflect an age of the island yet unformed and beyond thought. And the island itself, mother of these stones, lies here, standing firm against the sea and the wind, seemingly a fortress of the determinate holding those sweeping indeterminate forces at bay. The cliffs stark against the sky look like solidity itself, the original mold from which our image of an unchanging Being is formed. But their relation to the wind and the sea is much more complex than it might seem; the cliffs are not, after all, independent and immovable. Their lines of definition, starkly marked out as they may be at this moment or that, actually change in small ways and large, as the forces that seem so separate from them act over ages to carve and form the very boundaries that will then for a time hold firm against them. Here, in the play between the two, there is a creative energy that will give rise to new definitions and boundaries, but that can never be contained by any of them, the maps of which we grow so fond capturing only moments of this timeless play. So are the determinate lines of our categories and principles shaped and reformed as we mark them out against the restless indeterminacy of the world we seek to understand, understanding it each time a little better than the last, but beginning now to recognize that the conception of a completely determinate understanding is itself hopelessly incomplete.

INDEX